Nazi REGALIA

𝕹azi REGALIA

E. W. W. FOWLER

CHARTWELL
BOOKS, INC.

Published by
CHARTWELL BOOKS INC.
A Division of BOOK SALES, INC.
110 Enterprise Avenue
Secaucus, New Jersey 07094

Produced by Brompton Books Corp.
15 Sherwood Place
Greenwich, CT 06830

ISBN 1-55521-767-2

Printed in Hong Kong

PAGE 1: A dramatic wartime recruiting poster, showing a soldier carrying the *Reichskriegflagge*.

PAGE 2: Hitler, surrounded by his loyalest supporters, most in full-dress uniforms, National Workers' Day 1935.

PAGE 3: From left, an army NCO's cap, an officer's cap, and the hat of an SS general.

BELOW: Göring heads a parade of SA and SS troops, Nuremberg, 1934.

CONTENTS

THE NAZI PARTY 1919-1933

The Nazi Party or *Nationalsozialistische Deutsche Arbeiterpartei* (NSDAP), which was to traumatically change the face of Europe in six violent years, had its origins in the chaotic years in Germany following the defeat of November 1918. In 1919 Anton Drexler, Dietrich Eckart, and Karl Harrer set up the German Workers' Party *(Deutsche Arbeiterpartei)* in Munich. Adolf Hitler, a disgruntled former junior NCO, became its seventh member and persuaded the small group to hold a meeting at the Hofbrauhaus beer hall in Munich in November 1919. It was here that this frustrated artist discovered that he had a gift for oratory. His technique used a mix of abuse against the enemies who had betrayed the soldiers at the front, dire threats, and promises of retribution and the rebirth of a new and powerful Germany. By December there was a permanent office and Hitler was demanding better organization. By February 1920 Hitler had teamed with Drexler and Fedor to produce the '25 Points' which won them new supporters.

In April 1920 the party changed its name to NSDAP. It attracted men like Alfred Rosenberg, a refugee Baltic German who brought with him ideas of anti-semitism, racism and anti-Bolshevism; Captain Ernst Röhm, a tough serving soldier, joined with soldiers and members of the Freikorps. In October Emil Maurice began to organize Freikorps members into groups to keep order at the Nazi Party meetings. Dubbed 'Storm

PREVIOUS PAGES: The early days of the Nazi Party – a rally in Munich in January 1923.

ABOVE: Alfred Rosenberg the 'philosopher' of Nazi thought.

RIGHT: Hitler addresses an early meeting of the NSDAP.

BELOW LEFT: The swastika beside the traditional German Iron Cross on Hero's Memorial Day, March 16, 1941, in Berlin.

BELOW RIGHT: Hitler at a Nazi Party Brown Shirt (SA) rally in the 1920s.

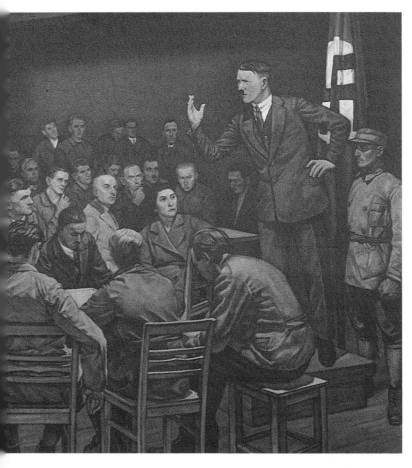

Groups' after the First World War raiding parties that attacked Allied positions in the trench warfare of 1914 – 1918, the *Sturmabteilung* or SA were to be a potent force in the street politics of the 1920s and 1930s.

By December Hitler had begun to move away from the old party committee and built up contacts with richer and more influential people. Röhm, Hess and Göring joined the party and General Ludendorff (the war hero) was alerted to the possibilities of the small nationalist political party.

The 25 Points

1. The union of all Germans in a Greater Germany.
2. The rejection of the Treaty of Versailles and the affirmation of the right of Germany to deal with other nations.
3. The demand for additional territories for food production and to settle excess German population: 'Lebensraum'.
4. Citizenship to be determined by race; no Jew to be a German.
5. Non-Germans in Germany to be only guests subject to appropriate foreign laws.
6. Official posts to be filled only according to character and qualification, not by political nepotism.
7. The livelihood of citizens to be the state's first duty. Should the state's resources be overstretched, non-citizens to be excluded from the state's benefits.
8. Non-German immigration to be stopped.
9. Equal rights and duties for all citizens.
10. Each citizen to work for the general good.
11. All income not earned by work to be confiscated.
12. All war profits to be confiscated.
13. All large business trusts to be nationalized.
14. Profit-sharing in all larger industries.
15. Adequate provision for old age.
16. Small businessmen and traders to be strengthened and large department stores to be handed over to them.
17. Reform of land-ownership and an end to land speculation.
18. Ruthless prosecution of serious criminals and death for profiteers.
19. Roman law, which is materialist, to be replaced by 'German law'.
20. A thorough reconstruction of the national education system.
21. The state to assist motherhood and encourage the development of the young.
22. The abolition of the paid professional army and the formation of a national army.
23. Newspapers must be German-owned; non-Germans banned from working on them.
24. Religious freedom, except for religions which endanger the German race; the party does not bind itself exclusively to any creed, but to fight against Jewish materialism.
25. A strong central government for the execution of effective legislation.

LEFT: The NSDAP Party Day in Nuremberg in August 1927. It is interesting to see the World War I decorations worn by Hitler and SA officers. Hess, the deputy Führer on Hitler's right, wears an SS cap.

RIGHT: Reichsführer SS Heinrich Himmler with the man he destroyed in the 'Night of the Long Knives,' Ernst Röhm, head of the SA. Röhm, who had a respectable military career in World War I, wears the Iron Cross First Class (EK1) and the wound badge. Himmler wears the striking and sinister black uniform of the prewar SS.

1921 saw Hitler gain total control of the party and become a recognized force in Bavarian politics. A year later Mussolini seized power in Italy and provided a dramatic example of Fascist power. The imagery of the Italian Fascists with black-shirted supporters, the raised arm salute and the title *Duce*, 'Leader', had an important influence on Hitler and the Nazi Party.

The following year Hitler was able to call on 70,000 party members and decided to gamble on a *putsch* in Munich. Led by Ludendorff and Hitler, the *putsch* foundered because it was not supported by the army or the current Bavarian government. The Nazi Party and SA were banned and Hitler jailed in Landsberg. Ironically, the *putsch*, in which a small number of Nazis were shot and killed by the army, provided the Nazi Party with a powerful icon, including the 'blood flag' – a swastika flag stained with the blood of the 'martyrs' – and a date to celebrate in later rallies. Hitler's term in Landsberg gave him time to dictate to Rudolf Hess his political testament, *Mein Kampf*, or 'My Fight.' He was released from Landsberg in December 1924 but the NSDAP was in ruins.

The following year was a tough one for Hitler as the party was banned from public meetings. Röhm resigned when Hitler refused to allow the SA to be separate from the Nazi Party.

However, in the summer of of 1924 the first unit of the SS was founded; the *Schutzstaffeln* were first intended to be a body guard for Hitler. Originally a small hand-picked group, by 1929, when Heinrich Himmler became Reichsführer SS, membership stood at 280. In June 1944 the Waffen SS numbered 594,000, the Allgemeine SS 200,000, and the Totenkopfverbände 24,000. In October that year there were 38 SS Divisions in the field with a total strength of 910,000 men. For many people the SS remain the definitive image of Nazi Germany. In the prewar days they wore a black uniform with silver fittings, and black boots and equipment. With the coming of war there was a move to field gray which made the Waffen SS look similar to the army, and men of the Allgemeine SS, who undertook the administration, security and counter-terrorism, were also keen to move away from the original, rather theatrical uniform. The sinister Totenkopfverbände, who ran the concentration camps, were also dressed in field gray. All retained the unique SS rank insignia and structure.

Returning to the mid-1920s, Hitler published the first part of *Mein Kampf* in 1925, and in Berlin a dynamic man named Josef Goebbels began to boost support for an old campaigner, Gregor Strasser. At the close of the year, however, Strasser openly challenged Hitler and even published a new party program replacing the 25 Points.

At the meeting at Bamberg in February 1926, Hitler outmaneuvered Strasser and won over Goebbels. In July that year the first Party rally was held at Weimar. The new salute of an outstretched arm was used for the first time by 5000 uniformed men. Party membership had grown to 27,000 and a Hitler Jugend (Hitler Youth) branch of the SA was formed. By November that year membership of the NSDAP was at 49,000. Goebbels had become Gauleiter of Berlin, a city with a strong Socialist and Communist tradition, while Rudolf Hess was made Party Secretary. At the end of the year the second volume of *Mein Kampf* was published.

In July 1927 the first of the Nuremberg Party Rallies was held. It was claimed that 30,000 uniformed SA men were present and Party membership had reached 70,000. Göring returned from Sweden and rejoined the Party for 'old comradeship and action' not, in his words, 'ideological junk'. In Berlin Goebbels held large meetings in which he insisted on the approaching end of the bourgeois state and gave vent to anti-semitic views.

In the 1928 elections for the Reichstag, the Nazis won 12 seats. Party membership passed 100,000 and its organization was divided into 34 Gau (regions), with seven more in areas considered 'German' like Austria and Danzig. In November Goebbels took over direction of propaganda from Strasser. Goebbels was a remarkable man who, despite a crippled left leg from a childhood illness, and a Rhineland working class family background, won scholarships and a university grant. He gained a doctorate in philology at Heidelberg University in 1921, and his resonating voice and powerful

oratory became a major asset for the Nazi Party. When Horst Wessel, a young SA fighter, was killed in a brawl in a prostitute's bedroom in February 1930 the details were hushed up and a simple marching song he had composed became, under Goebbels' patronage, almost the second national anthem of Germany. The 'Horst Wessel' song is a *leitmotif* behind Leni Riefenstahl's film *Triumph des Willens* (Triumph of the Will), the powerful film of the Nazi Party Congress in Nuremberg in September 1934.

LEFT: Goebbels, head of the Propaganda Ministry, talks to a young member of the Hitler Youth.

BELOW LEFT: The Leibstandarte-SS 'Adolf Hitler' (Hitler's SS bodyguard) parade past the Führer on his birthday on April 20 1938. The band in the foreground have the characteristic German 'swallows nests' shoulder insignia for bands and standard bearers.

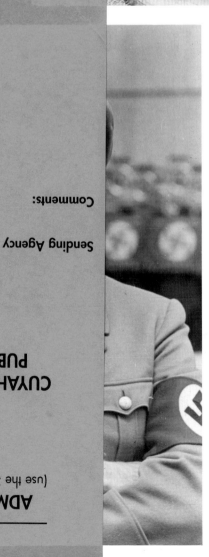

LEFT: The 1934 Nuremberg Rally. Hitler stands next to Himmler and Lutze, Röhm's successor as head of the SA after the 'Night of the Long Knives'.

BELOW: SA men carrying party colors.

RIGHT: Hitler at the Templehof field in Berlin on May 1 1934. While the SA may outnumber the black uniformed SS, it is the SS who are the bodyguard for the Führer. The SS Gruppenführer accompanying Hitler on the right is wearing the 'Holbein' dagger adopted by both the SA and the SS.

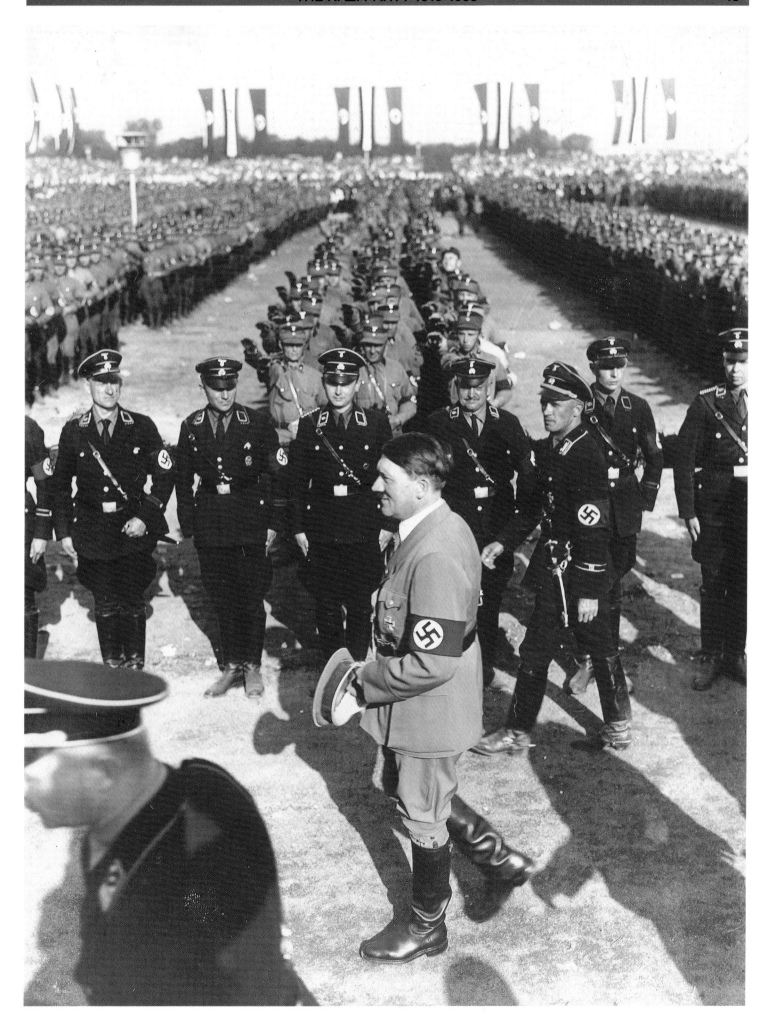

LEFT: An early Nazi Party rally in the 1920s, with SA Storm Troopers in an almost civilian uniform. Distinctive in the foreground is an SA banner.

BELOW LEFT: SA men, with black arm bands covering their swastika *kampfbinde*, stand guard over the grave of Horst Wessel in November 1934.

RIGHT: The meeting in the Luitpoldhalle at the 1933 Nuremberg Rally. Swastikas and eagles are used to theatrical effect.

BELOW: With Sepp Dietrich at the wheel of the Mercedes, Hitler reaches out to shake hands with admirers at Buckeberg in 1934. Dietrich's role as driver earned him the nickname of 'Chauffeureska'.

The Nazis gained 107 seats in elections for the Reichstag in September 1930. This put them second after the SDP who had 143 seats; the Communists had 77. The SA, now at 100,000, was larger than the German regular army. A year later Röhm returned from Bolivia where he had been working as a military instructor and took command of the SA. In 1932 Hitler's ambitions were becoming evident – in presidential elections he ran against Hindenburg, a World War I general who was greatly respected by many Germans. The result was close, with Hindenburg winning 49.6 percent of the vote and Hitler 30 percent. However, this was not an absolute majority and a new election was necessary. The SA, now a massive 400,000-strong force was mobilized in Berlin, and there were fears that there would be a *putsch*. A month later the SA was banned and in a second election Hindenburg was re-elected, despite the fact that Hitler gained more votes.

Von Papen was elected Chancellor and lifted the ban on the SA in June. A month later in the Reichstag elections the Nazis won 230 seats, making them the largest party, but without an overall majority. In a ceremony full of bitter irony Clara Zetkin, a veteran Communist, and oldest delegate to the Reichstag, presided over the election of Göring as its President.

Confident that he held the political initiative, Hitler mobilized the SA in August and demanded the Chancellorship from the President: Hindenburg refused. The Nazis teamed with the Communists in a Berlin transport strike in October and this demonstration of political street power lost the Nazis valuable seats in elections in November.

As parties from the center and left struggled to retain power, they were unable to keep a working majority. In January 1933 a cabinet which had Hitler as Chancellor, von Papen as Vice-Chancellor and three Nazis holding ministerial posts, was cobbled together. This was a critical year: after the Reichstag fire in February, Hindenburg signed a decree suspending civil rights, and there were mass arrests of communists, socialists and liberals. The SA, working as police auxiliaries, were drafted in to conduct arrests. Earlier that month industrialists and financiers had agreed to back the Nazis as the party most likely to save the country from a slide into disorder – there was a feeling that the unsophisticated Nazi politicians could be manipulated and controlled. However, earlier that month the Nazis had already shown that they were adept at manipulation, when a raid on the Communist Party headquarters produced papers that proved the Communists were planning a revolution.

In March 1933 the last Reichstag elections were held and the Nazis won 288 seats; this was not an absolute majority, so they teamed with Hugenberg's 52 nationalist DNVP delegates. With all 81 Communist members and a large number of Socialists barred from the Reich-

stag, Hitler held a strong enough majority to alter the constitution. Through the process of *Gleichschaltung*, the co-ordination or unification of the Reich, he introduced the Third Reich.

It took less than a year for the Nazis to take complete control of Germany. Opposition parties were banned and the civil service, unions, and legal system of Germany were taken over. A retrospective law passed on March 29 gave sanction for the hanging of the weak-minded Dutchman named Marius van Lubbe who had been accused of starting the Reichstag fire.

Hitler styled his new government the Third Reich; the first Reich (or Empire) was the Holy Roman Empire which lasted from 800 to its abolition by Napoleon in 1806. The second Reich was Bismarck's which lasted from 1871 to the end of the Hohenzollern dynasty in 1918. Hitler boasted that the Third Reich would last for a thousand years.

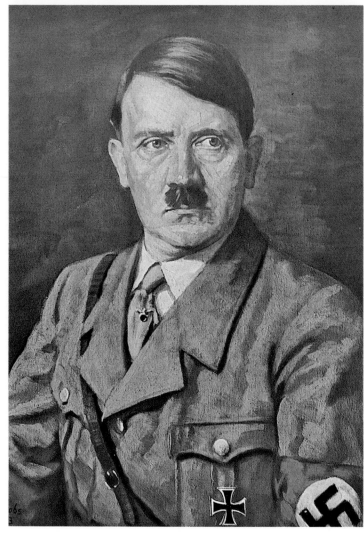

Though Hitler had eliminated his external enemies he was still faced by the SA which, under Röhm, was a powerful organization of half a million, and larger than the army. Meanwhile, the SA had to watch as the Prussian secret police, the *GEheimes STAatsPOlizei* or Gestapo, was taken over by Himmler's SS. Under Himmler the SS were a small, but very loyal armed and uniformed guard for Hitler and the Nazi leaders – they soon became an instrument of political violence.

The army and traditionalists – even von Papen, the Deputy Chancellor – were pressing for action against the SA. The Röhm Purge, Blood Purge, or Night of the Long Knives, which over the night of Saturday June 30 and Sunday July 1 1933 eliminated the SA leadership, was preceded by a build up of tension which began with

ABOVE LEFT: Hitler and Röhm stand shoulder to shoulder in September 1933. Nine months later Röhm would be dead, killed by an SS squad.

LEFT: The 1933 Jacobs portrait of Hitler. The Führer was one of the most widely photographed, filmed and painted national leaders of the twentieth century.

RIGHT: A *Reichsadler* straddles the slogan 'Blut und Boden' (Blood and Soil), in a poster for the fifth Reichs Farmers' Day at Goslar. The Nazis wrapped up their ideology in mythical language relating to superior Nordic races and 'Pure Blood'.

von Papen's speech at Marburg on June 10. On June 26 senior SS officers were informed by Himmler that the SA planned a revolt. A day later Sepp Dietrich, a former warrant officer in the army during the First World War, who now commanded the SS guard detachment in Berlin, went to the army to collect extra weapons and transport. He pressed his demand by showing the army officer with whom he was speaking an 'SA execution list' which included the officer's name.

Three days later the *Völkischer Beobachter* (the Party newspaper) published an article by Field Marshal Werner von Blomberg the Minister of Defense, which pledged loyalty to Hitler but demanded curbs to the power of the SA. Hitler visited labor camps and then went to his favorite Rhine village of Bad Godesberg near Bonn where he was joined by Goebbels. In Berlin Göring mobilized his police and SS units.

On the morning of the 30th Hitler flew to Munich with Goebbels, his press chief Dietrich, and Lutze of the SA. Lutze, the SA leader in Hanover, had reported Röhm's demands that the SA be given the primary role of defending Germany. Lutze was to survive the Röhm Purge to become the head of the SA – now a relatively powerless organization.

In Munich Hitler ordered the SA officers Schmidt and Schneidhuber to Stadelheim jail, shouting that they would be shot. The Gauleiter was given a list of SA men and other 'enemies' in Bavaria who were to be arrested. Hitler then drove to Bad Weisse where Röhm and other SA men were staying; they were ordered to Stadelheim with the exception of Heines, the SA commander of Silesia, who was discovered in bed with his boyfriend and was shot immediately. In Berlin Goebbels sent the unlikely code-word, 'Colibri' – Humming Bird – and with prompt ruthlessness the SS took SA leaders to the army cadet school at Lichterfelde and shot them. At the Brown House in Munich Hitler prepared announcements explaining the reason for the purge.

On Sunday July 1 Hitler attended a public function. Since Röhm had refused to commit suicide with a pistol that had been prepared and, indeed, had said that if he was to die Hitler should execute him, Hitler gave the order. An SS squad led by Theodore Eicke, a man who was later to perfect the concentration camp system, went to Röhm's cell and murdered him.

On the 13th Hitler spoke at the Reichstag and explained why the actions against the SA had been necessary. He claimed that only 19 senior and 42 other SA men had been shot, while 13 others had died resisting

arrest, with three committing suicide. The reality was that probably more than 1000 died – enemies included Nazis who did not fit the new mold and, by accident, a music critic called Schmid who had the same name as an SA leader. Intriguingly, Father Stempfle, an old Nazi, was killed – possibly because he knew too much about Hitler's relationship with his niece Geli Raubal.

Having removed the threat of the SA, only the conservative leaders of the army posed a threat to Hitler. Hitler and his security services adroitly used the very conservative values of these officers to destroy them and so give Hitler control over the army. Field Marshal Werner von Blomberg, the Minister of Defense from 1933 to 1938, took a personal oath of loyalty to Hitler and delivered the army into Hitler's hands. Göring encouraged the widowed von Blomberg to marry a young woman, Erna Grun; he was then able to produce Grun's police record as a prostitute, with pornographic photographs to back up his allegations. Hitler was able to force Blomberg to resign and took the role of Minister of Defense himself.

The army Commander-in-Chief under Blomberg, General Freiherr Werner von Fritsch, welcomed the rise to power of the Nazis but expressed reservations about the power of the SS as well as the plans to invade Austria and Czechoslovakia. The SS framed von Fritsch in 1938 with allegations by a petty criminal that the general had been seen in the company of a male prostitute. Fritsch was cashiered from the army. In a secret army court of honor he was found not guilty – the homosexual officer seen by the criminal existed, however: he was an elderly cavalry captain named Frisch. In 1939 von Fritsch rejoined his old regiment as honorary colonel and was killed in fighting in Poland.

Thus, by the beginning of the Second World War Hitler, who had started adult life as a failed painter and junior NCO in the First World War, was in total control of a powerful, united and heavily industrialized nation.

ADOLF HITLER

FÜHRER   KANZLER

DEUTSCHES   REICH

REICHS - KANZLER

HITLER MAG DIE KINDER GERNE

HEIL HITLER!

ABOVE LEFT: Himmler and Sepp Dietrich take the salute in summer 1940. The Waffen SS has been in action in Poland and France and Dietrich has added new decorations to those he won in World War I.

LEFT: Decorations for Hitler's 50th birthday at an NSDAP office in Worms.

TOP RIGHT: A poster which announces 'Hitler loves children', shows the swastika and the older red, white and black flag.

RIGHT: Hitler, Goebbels and Franz von Papen, the Vice-Chancellor, (on Hitler's right) in 1933.

Neisse
Hohenbaden
Heilbron
UTSCHLAND
ERWACHE
DEUTSCHLAND
ERWACHE
DEUTSCHLA
ERWACHE

THE TOTEMS
OF POWER

There had always been a fascination with the respect and dignity associated with uniforms and rank in Germany, dating from before the First World War. After 1918, with the Kaiser in exile in Holland, and the army reduced to a tiny security force, many of the exotic Imperial uniforms disappeared. The Nazis brought back uniforms in variety and volume and with them the insignia and trappings of power.

The most powerful symbol of the Nazis was the swastika or hooked cross. Even before it was adopted by Hitler, it had nationalistic and anti-semitic provenance in Germany. The Ehrhardt Freikorps Brigade, which operated in Germany in the confused private wars of the early 1920s, painted large swastikas on their helmets. The swastika was originally a Hindu symbol from India, but in this form it stood square and the hooks faced to the left; the word itself is derived from the Sanskrit *su* meaning 'well' and *asti* meaning 'being'. Hitler faced the hooks to the right and tilted the cross on its side as a representation of movement – there was a legend that turning the swastika back to front would bring bad luck to the instigator.

Hitler saw it as an 'Aryan' symbol and incorporated it into the new national flag in 1935. In the strange racial fantasies of Nazi Germany, 'Aryan' represented an ideal of Nordic-German racial purity. It fostered a bizarre form of academic research into Nordic runes, mythology and symbolism. One of the by-products of this study was runic devices for Waffen SS and Nazi Party uniforms and even vehicles. The 'sun wheel' version of the swastika had the outer arms of the cross curved, and was adopted by the 11.SS-Freiwilligen-Panzer-Grenadier-Division 'Nordland', though it was also used in insignia like the anti-partisan badge. Adopting a runic style, the letters SS were produced as two parallel lightning flashes and were to become a

PREVIOUS PAGES: The 'Blood Flag' ceremony in the Luitpold Arena in Nuremberg in September 1934.

ABOVE: Men of the Leibstandarte stand in front of the Führer as he speaks to the Hitler Youth at the Templehof Field, Berlin.

LEFT: Hitler in 1933. He wears the Iron Cross First Class and Wound Badge – he was gassed in the First World War.

ABOVE RIGHT: Bicycle-mounted SA pass Hitler in a parade in Dortmund.

RIGHT: The Brown House in Munich. In almost religious symbolism, swastika standards have been gathered together. The Brown House on Briennerstrasse was the NSDAP headquarters.

symbol second only to the swastika in menace and power during Hitler's years in power.

All the totalitarian states – fascist Italy and Soviet Russia – adopted symbols. The Italians with the lictor's bundle of rods – the fasces – showed the symbolism of strength in unity, while the Soviet Union had the red star or the hammer and sickle, the latter representing industry and agriculture.

The swastika was incorporated into the red, white and black national colors, which were first adopted for the national cockade in 1897 as the emblem of the German Empire. As an arm band – black swastika on white circle on a red arm band – it was a potent symbol which could be worn with civilian clothes or as part of a uniform. Later, in the early years of the war, the red flag with a swastika was a useful air identification panel for fast-moving German armored vehicles as they punched into Scandanavia, France and the Low Countries, the Balkans and the Soviet Union, as well as the sands of North Africa. It was attached to the rear deck of vehicles or even laid out in patterns on the front line.

Officially this flag was the trade ensign, but was upgraded in 1935 to the status of the German National Flag. At the prewar Nuremberg political rallies, massed swastika flags were used very effectively, producing a sea of red, black and white. The swastika was also employed to emphasize the unity of the Third Reich, while regional flags were phased out.

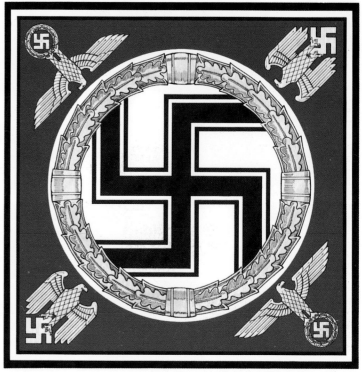

Hitler's personal standard as Führer and Chancellor of the German Nation was square with a narrow black and white border; there was an oak leaf wreath on a red field within which was a 'static' swastika, set square, and in opposite corners were a *Reichsadler* and *Wehrmachtadler*.

The *Oberkommando der Wehrmacht* (Armed Forces High Command) had a red swallow-tailed flag with a narrow black and white border. In the center was a conventional swastika; an iron cross, and beneath it a *Reichsadler*, were positioned next to the vertical edge.

Standards and colors carried by units of the German army bore an iron cross, at the center of which was a silver oak wreath with a black *Reichsadler* on a white background within. The flags had a silver fringing and regimental streamers. The background color was in the *Waffenfarbe* of the unit and in each corner was a small swastika. Most flags were swallow-tailed, although Jäger (Light Infantry), Engineer and Infantry flags were square. Standard bearers had distinctive sleeve insignia which showed a *Reichsadler* flanked by flags with five oak leaf fronds at the base and also wore a gorget. Many of the German flags were captured by the Soviet army at the end of the war and in a dramatic piece of theater, paraded in 1945 in Red Square, Moscow. At a command, the Soviet soldiers then threw them down at the steps of Lenin's mausoleum.

FAR LEFT: Hitler attends Wagner's *Meistersinger* at the Nuremberg opera house. The *Führerstandarte*, the personal standard for Adolf Hitler as Führer, hangs in front of the box.

LEFT: The *Führerstandarte*, showing the *Reichsadler* and *Wehrmachtadler*, as well as the oak leaf wreath.

BELOW LEFT: The swastika and death's head incorporated into early NSDAP banners.

RIGHT: SS troops carrying party banners which bear the old Nazi slogan 'Deutschland Erwache' (Germany awake). The prewar SS were regarded by the army as fit only for parades.

BELOW RIGHT: A spread of army Regimental Standard Bearers' armshields. The arm colors (*Waffenfarben*) indicate the unit: pink for panzers; yellow, signals; black, engineers; white, infantry; red, artillery; and apple green, panzer grenadiers.

LEFT: Hitler with General von Blomberg, Göring, General von Fritsch and Admiral Raeder at Nuremberg in 1935. Hitler destroyed the careers of the two generals and thus the power of the army.

BELOW LEFT: SA troops stand with their banners, watching Hitler on the podium at the Luitpold Arena. The SA dagger can be seen on the belt of the man on the right.

BELOW: The Führer's standard is to the right of the podium above the massed ranks of SA in 1938.

RIGHT: The exhilaration of the Victory Parade in Berlin in 1940 following the defeat of France, the Netherlands, Belgium, Norway and Poland. Camera crews record this high point in Hitler's career.

LEFT: Half-tracked artillery prime movers roar past the Führer while a huge *Reichsadler* looms over the audience.

RIGHT: Party leaders and local worthies, some with World War I decorations, grouped around a pre-Nazi banner, which has been discreetly draped with a small swastika.

BELOW: An NSDAP political leader's arm band and collar patches. Prewar designs like these were in high quality velvet with metal fittings.

The swastika arm band worn on the upper left sleeve was a prominent part of every uniform in prewar Germany. The basic design was similar to the national flag with the symbol enclosed within a white disc against a red background. However, the *Hitler Jugend*, Hitler Youth, the Nazi youth movement which swallowed up all the German youth movements when the Nazis came to power, had an arm band which had a broad white bar running through it and the swastika enclosed within a square. The NSD, *Studenten Bund*, the German students' union had an arm band with the swastika compressed into a diamond shape and a white bar above and below the insignia running left to right. The SS had the standard arm band (or SS-*Kampfbinde*) but with a black stripe as a border at the top and bottom. On service dress the arm band was made from a heavy wool material, while on summer-weight shirts it was made in cotton. For a short time members of the SS who had been elected to the Reichstag wore the *Reichstagabgeordneter* (member of the Reichstag arm band), a distinctive version which had two stripes of gold tress enclosed within the black stripes. There are also examples of an unattributed SS arm band with black and white piping in place of the black border.

The swastika was combined with the eagle – a bird which Hitler regarded as Aryan – and in various forms appeared on everything from coinage, through uniforms to massive bronze statuary. The most common designs were either with wings spread or partly folded. The origins of the eagle as a German national emblem can be traced back to 800 when Charlemagne was crowned emperor in Rome and adopted the eagle which had been carried by the Roman legions. The spread eagle can be traced back to 1100, the period of the Hohenstaufen dynasty. The revolutionaries of 1848, the German Second Reich of 1871, and the Weimar Republic of 1919 all adopted the earlier single-headed spread eagle symbol.

The spread eagle with its head aligned to the right, appeared clasping an oak leaf wreath-ringed swastika on all military uniforms. The oak wreath was adopted by many military forces in Europe since the oak symbolized strength – similarly laurels were used as the symbol of victory, an icon which could be traced back to the Greeks who garlanded sporting and military triumphs.

The *Heer* (army) and *Kriegsmarine* (navy) had the *Wehrmachtadler,* an insignia on the left breast of the tunic and a smaller version on caps and head dress above the older traditional red, white and black cockade. As the war progressed the woven aluminum thread badges were replaced by mass-produced versions. The firm of BeVo pioneered these machine-embroidered artificial silk badges and their name became synonymous with mass-produced late-war badges.

The SS, however, moved the eagle to their left sleeve and produced a modified version. The insignia was first officially introduced for wear in May 1936, although the *Ärmelhoheitsabzeichen,* or National Emblem for the Sleeve, was already being worn by Sepp Dietrich as early as the summer of 1935. The SS eagle was almost identical to the army bird, except for the outer edge of the wings. Interestingly Hitler wore an eagle on his sleeve, but adopted the army version.

In a world that became obsessed with insignia and the trappings of power, it is worth digressing here to look at the decorations worn by Hitler. As Führer, he wore his Iron Cross First Class (EK1) which was proof of front line bravery, awarded in August 1918. He had previously won the Iron Cross Second Class in 1914. Other medals awarded to him in the First World War were a Military Cross Third Class with Swords in September 1917, the Regimental Award for Outstanding Bravery, and the Medal for the Wounded both in May 1918, and the Service Medal, Third Class in August 1918. Hitler's decision to wear only the EK1 was in marked contrast to Göring who, though he had won the coveted *Pour le Mérite* (nicknamed the Blue Max, it was an elegant blue

ABOVE: The German army year book for 1941 which bears the *Wehrmachtadler.*

ABOVE LEFT: A German soldier's pay book which contained details of training, issued equipment and postings.

LEFT: The Reichscockade cap badge and *Reichsadler* (center), with BeVo-quality breast eagles.

ABOVE RIGHT: Göring wearing the *Pour le Mérite* and Knight's Cross, which were dwarfed by the vulgar Grand Cross of which he was the only recipient.

RIGHT: The 1940 Victory Parade when Hitler and Göring were still good friends. Göring wears the Knight's Cross, *Pour le Mérite*, the Pilot's Badge and the Iron Cross First Class for World War I and II. Hitler's simpler uniform has an army-style *Wehrmachtadler* on the left sleeve in the SS style. The young SS officer in the background with ADC's aiguillettes is Max Wunsche.

FAR LEFT: The Brandenburg Gate, floodlit and swastika-draped. Through this gate in central Berlin, triumphant German armies paraded in the early years of the war.

ABOVE LEFT: A vintage with a message, swastikas on the label on a bottle of white wine.

LEFT: A man's neck tie with swastika motifs.

BOTTOM LEFT: An Aryan eagle wings towards a National Socialist dawn.

BELOW: SA and SS dagger hangers which combine national colors and political motifs.

LEFT: Tie clips and a necklace for the Party faithful. Black, white and red or the swastika are the dominant theme.

BELOW: The propagandist's view of the progression from Hitler Youth to SS.

BELOW LEFT: A recruiting poster to encourage young German girls to join the Bund Deutscher Mädel (League of German girls).

BUND DEUTSCHER MÄDEL IN DER HITLER JUGEND

enamel cross which was Imperial Germany's highest decoration), developed a taste for exotic decorations and uniforms. However, while Göring was a commissioned fighter ace in the First World War, Hitler was a mere corporal, so wearing all his decorations would have drawn attention to his humble background. During the Second World War senior German officers called Hitler 'the Bavarian Corporal', behind his back.

Göring's Luftwaffe, which included the paratroop arm and later ground forces with armor, had an eagle with wings curved in flight clutching a swastika in its talons. It was similar in some respects to the RAF eagle, though the RAF were quick to point out that their's was flying to the left, while the Luftwaffe version flew (rather aptly) to the right.

The other eagle insignia was the *Reichsadler* or Reich Eagle, which had its wings partly open; as a design this version was a square shape, while the eagle with open wings was more oblong. The eagle with semi-opened wings appeared on coins and official notices and literature. It was also reproduced in bronze in massive sculptures at many of the Nazi public buildings.

The swastika and eagle also appeared on the belt buckles of soldiers of the *Heer* – the buckle retained the circular wreath with the motto GOTT MIT UNS – 'God With Us,' which had been worn by soldiers in the First World War. (During the Christmas truce in the trenches in 1914 a British officer, having asked a German what the motto meant, replied with surprise and shock 'Oh no, He's with *us*').

The First World War buckle had featured the Imperial crown as its center, and in the Second this was replaced by an eagle and swastika. Officers retained a Sam Browne-style belt with an open double claw buckle, though in full-dress they had a buckle with an eagle and

FAR LEFT: Göring in Luftwaffe mess kit, with the elegant Count Galeazzo Ciano, the Italian Foreign Minister, and the German Foreign Minister, von Neurath in 1936.

ABOVE LEFT: German currency bore the *Reichsadler* device.

BELOW LEFT: A postwar photograph shows the uniform of an SS-Untersturmführer of the SS-Regiment Deutschland wearing the EK 1 and army Flak Badge.

ABOVE: The uniform of SS-Obergruppenführer (General) Oswald Pohl, who was chief of the Economic and Administrative Central office of the SS.

RIGHT: Göring and Albert Kesselring. Göring has secured his summer-pattern cap with its chin strap.

swastika surrounded by an oak wreath, but without the motto. The SS, as is to be expected, had their own design for buckles. For other ranks the wreath and eagle were retained, but the eagle had fully-spread wings surmounting the wreath and holding a swastika in its claws within a smaller wreath. The officers' buckle had a similar open-winged eagle and interestingly, both had a swastika set square rather than the accepted Nazi version at an angle. The most significant feature of the SS buckles was the motto. The SS had adopted a non-Christian ethic since Christianity was perceived as having Jewish origin, so their motto, which also appeared on the blade of their dress daggers, could not

include the word 'God'. Instead it read MEINE EHRE HEISST TREUE – 'My Honor is Loyalty'; this loyalty was to be tested as the victorious first months of the Second World War turned into a series of grim fighting retreats across Europe to the Reich. The same motto appeared on the SS dagger and officers' swords. The dagger was similar to that worn by the SA and NSKK except that the scabbard was black and had the SS runes close to the pommel. The SS honor dagger had German silver guards and a damascus steel blade with the SS motto raised and gilded.

The SA had a variety of buckle designs, all with the eagle, swastika and wreath, but some with the swastika

LEFT: The National War Flag which was introduced on November 7 1935.

BELOW LEFT: *Deutsche Jungvolk*, the junior version of the *Hitlerjugend* (HJ) prepare for a march in 1939.

RIGHT: The elegant Mother's Cross which was awarded in three classes to mothers with four to five children, six to seven and eight or more. The Second Class in silver and the First Class in gold.

FAR RIGHT: *Hitlerjugend* drummers march through a German town. Hitler was fascinated by the idea of a new generation of hard young men who would be molded into good soldiers.

set square, others with its hooked arms curved and, for senior officers with the SA, initials in an ingenious pseudo-runic design mid-center on the eagle's breast.

The swastika was also used to alter military and civil decorations. The Iron Cross was established on March 10 1813 when Friedrich Wilhelm III of Prussia inaugurated a decoration which could be awarded regardless of rank. It originally featured a crown at its center, but under the Nazis the crown was replaced by a swastika and the date 1939, marking the beginning of the Second World War – just as decorations from an earlier war bore the date 1914 . Its design was rooted in tradition and could, however, be traced back to a black cross adopted by German crusaders between 1074 and 1270. The cross was used on war flags in the 19th century and reinstated by the Nazi government in a new flag in November 1935.

The *Reichskriegsflagge* became the ensign of the German armed forces and was flown from warships, over barracks and used for formal ceremonies. It consisted of a red rectangle with a swastika (its arms edged with a narrow black and white border), within a white disk surrounded by a black border placed off-center, closer to the mast. The disk was at the center of a cross with arms made up of four white and three black bars running to the borders of the flag. In the canton was an iron cross on a similarly spaced narrow white background.

Hitler introduced the flag with an order of the day:

Soldiers of the Armed Forces!

Today I give to the re-established Armed Forces the introduction of national conscription and the new National War Flag.

Let the Swastika be your symbol of unity and purity of the Nation, the sign of National Socialist ideology, the foundation of freedom and our country's strength.

The Iron Cross should remind you of the unique tradition of the old Army, of the ideals which inspired them, of the example that they have given you.

The National colors black, white and red bind you to loyal service in life and in death.
To follow the flag should be your pride.
The former War Flag shall be retired with honor. I reserve the right to order it to be flown on special occasions.

(Signed) The Führer and Supreme Commander-in-Chief of the Armed Forces, Adolf Hitler.

National Socialist from cradle to grave

After 1933 the Nazi government had not only take control of the armed forces, but also of the whole of German society. From cradle to grave a German man or woman would be part of a Nazi-controlled organization. At his or her birth a young German might qualify his mother for the *Ehrenkreuz der Deutschen Mutter,* the Cross of Honor of the German Mother. This elegant blue and white enamel cross was worn on a narrow blue and white ribbon. It came in three classes – the third in bronze was for a mother of four or five children, the second in silver was for six or seven and the first, which was gold-plated was for a hard-working mother of eight or more children. The idea behind the Mother's Cross was to encourage larger families to make up for the huge loss of manpower following the First World War. There were other compensations, including domestic help and tax assistance for large families.

At the age of six a child entered the *Volksschule* and at ten joined the *Deutsches Jungvolk,* or DJV, if a boy, and the *Deutsche Jungmädel,* or DJM, if a girl. A boy in

the DJV was known as a *'Pimpf'* and had to undergo an initiation test which included recalling points of Nazi dogma, reciting the *Horst Wessel* song, running 50 meters in 12 seconds, joining in two-day cross country hikes, practising semaphore and learning arms drill. During this period they became eligible for selection for the *Nationalpolitische Erziehungsanstalten* or NPEA, the National Political Education Institute, which was also known as the NAPOLA. If the child won a place at the NPEA or the Adolf Hitler Schools, they were on the way to becoming one of the Party élite, since the education system then took them to the *Ordensburgen*, or Castles of Order, and thence after party service, to the *Hohe Schule*, the Party Academy. The NPEA, which could trace its origins back to the Weimar Republic, and in some ways resembled military academies in the United States, was a success. A student at the NAPOLA wore an earth gray uniform which consisted of a four-pocket tunic and trousers. He had a mustard khaki shirt with black tie and brown facings on the tunic collar. This color was repeated in the cap band of the black peaked cap. On his left sleeve was an SS-style eagle. The epaulets were black and bore the letters NPEA. Officers also carried a distinctive dagger, which although similar to the SA, SS and NSKK 'Holbein' dagger whose design dated back to the 15th and 16th centuries, had an eagle and swastika on the grip and the motto MEHR SEIN ALS SCHEINEN – 'Be more than you appear to be.' Students retained their HJ knives.

In reality, although the *Ordensburgen* were created, the Party Academies were never constructed. The *Ordensburgen* were constructed in Pomerania, the Eifel, and Bavaria in remote, romantic settings. Part of their philosophy was a gothic fantasy of a knightly order steeped in discipline in a castellated academy towering over the surrounding countryside. Students or *Junkers* at the *Ordensburgen* wore a mustard khaki uniform with a brown belt. The cap had a brown peak and band and on the left sleeve was the name of the *Ordensburgen* – thus *Vogelsang* if he was attending the academy in the Eifel.

Ordinary mortals, however, entered grammar school at 12 and then joined the HJ, *Hitler Jugend* (Hitler Youth) or BDM *Bund Deutscher Mädel*, League of German Girls, at the age of 14, and membership lasted to the age of 18 or 19. Boys were entitled to carry the bayo-

net-style sheath knife with the slogan 'Blood and Honor'. Of all the edged weapons produced during the life of the Third Reich, the HJ knife was the most prolific. Between 1934 and 1945 over 20,000,000 were manufactured and after the war the makers continued production with the Boy Scout trefoil substituted for the swastika. The Hitler Youth was made compulsory for young people by the Hitler Youth Law of December

FAR LEFT: Members of a girls school salute the flag. They would have been members of the BDM, Bund Deutscher Mädel.

LEFT: BDM on the march, carrying the HJ flag and wearing the BDM uniform.

BELOW LEFT: BDM at war. This bicycle despatch rider has a civilian gas mask and her uniform has an HJ sleeve diamond.

TOP RIGHT: Hitler Youth (HJ) Flak helper's M43 cap. The HJ diamond is on the front where soldiers would have worn the eagle and swastika national emblem.

RIGHT: The prewar pattern HJ NCO's cap. The leather chin strap distinguishes it as NCO headgear.

BELOW: An HJ Flieger Officer cap – an intriguing combination of the army-pattern eagle, HJ diamond and Luftwaffe-pattern cap.

Alle 10jährigen zu uns

Herausgegeben von der Reichsjugendführung. Verantwortlich: Bannführer Lerche.   Hersteller: Jupp Daehler (Graphische Arbeitsgemeinscha

LEFT: 'All girls are one' – says the BDM poster. It emphasizes the Nazi ideal of a classless society reflecting the front line values of World War I. Women in the Nazi order always played a secondary role and their function could be summed up by the slogan 'Kinder, Kirche, Kuche' – Children, Church and Kitchen.

TOP RIGHT: Roses, roses all the way – BDM girls in summer uniforms strew flowers along the route used by soldiers marching in the 1940 Victory Parade in Berlin.

BELOW RIGHT: HJ Summer Service Dress. On the belt with its characteristic nickel HJ buckle, is the short bladed knife (*HJ-Fahrtenmesser*). The *HJ-Gebiete*, or district, can be seen in number form on the epaulet and in letters on the triangle on the sleeve. The small HJ diamond-shaped badge was sometimes worn as a breast badge by soldiers on their tunics.

1936 which banned all other youth organizations. In some ways the HJ was a radical organisation which aimed to take young people away from their social backgrounds and mix them together, giving boys from country backgrounds access to sports facilities normally only available to town dwellers.

The HJ featured in the film *Triumph des Willens* (Triumph of the Will), the powerful documentary by Leni Riefenstahl about the Nazi Party congress at Nuremberg in September 1934. The massed ranks of young musicians with their flame-decorated drums and trumpeters with runic banners, as well as the stadium filled with HJ, has a dramatic impact even on audiences in the late 20th century . The HJ wore a summer uniform of black shorts, a long-sleeved khaki mustard shirt, black neckerchief, a belt with cross strap, and black side cap with red piping. Epaulets and a colored triangular badge on the left sleeve showed the HJ region. (The HJ regional organization was based on the *Gebiete* further broken down into *Banne, Stamme, Gefolgschaften, Scharen* and *Kameradschaften*). The lower sleeve could also carry badges indicating skills that the young person might have acquired. Adult leaders wore a single-breasted, four-pocket khaki mus-

tard tunic with black trousers, and a peaked cap with the political eagle above the HJ diamond-shaped swastika insignia. Like the young members' uniforms, a black triangle on the left sleeve showed the region, and black epaulets displayed rank. A swastika arm band with the characteristic HJ design with a central white bar was won on the left sleeve. Girls wore a beige short-waisted jacket, white blouse with neckerchief and black skirt. Leaders and members had a belt buckle which displayed an eagle with its claws holding the triangular HJ swastika and above the motto, BLUT UND EHRE, 'Blood and Honor.' 'Blood' was a strongly Nazi concept which encapsulated racism, patriotism and loyalty to one's roots and origins. Boys would undertake route marches loaded with the packs, water bottles, shovels and mess tins like soldiers in the field. There were decorations for skill and merit; the *Hitler Jugend Ehrenabzeichen* (Hitler Youth Badge of Honor) came in two classes, the superior of which had an oak leaf border. The BDM and JM (*Jungmädel*) had discreet Honor Badges, which were brooches with the letters BDM or JM. There were also badges for riding and handling horse-drawn vehicles for both adults and young people – the HJ riding badge was simply a smaller version of the adult one. The Nazi 'thinkers' were fascinated by the unlikely idea of an Aryan German élite riding through their estates in the lands of eastern Europe. The HJ also instituted shooting awards for their members: the *Hitler Jugend schiessauszeichnungen* came in the classes Marksmanship, Sharpshooter (silver oak leaves) and Expert (gilt oak leaves).

LEFT: Hitler Youth and BDM proficiency and *Gau* insignia. The Luftwaffe eagle badge with letters FH was issued to Flak Helpers (anti-aircraft crews).

BELOW: The HJ armband and DJ proficiency badge. Both show the Nordic runic influence on design.

RIGHT: An HJ cuff title (top) and cuff titles from officials of one of the 43 *Gau* or districts set up by the Nazis when they took power. The *Gau* was also identical to a civil defense region; additional *Gaue* were set up with the annexation of Austria and Czechoslovakia.

BELOW RIGHT: The Führer's image on a pocket knife. Knives, daggers and cleavers were an important part of Nazi and military uniforms.

BELOW FAR RIGHT: SA and adult HJ members sing in a choir at the opening of the first German Song Week which lasted from 7 to 12 May 1934. Patriotic, sentimental and political songs were popular at NSDAP gatherings and throughout service life.

In *Triumph of the Will*, the parade of the Hitler Youth makes powerful cinema. Baldur von Schirach, the Reich Youth Leader, introduces Hitler to the massed ranks of the HJ with the words, 'Loyalty. We'll be loyal to you for ever and ever.' Hitler steps forward and in characteristically hesitant opening tones replies 'You are only part of the millions who are not here. You must educate yourself to obedience. Be peace-loving and brave. Don't be effeminate. Be hard and tough. Live austerely. We will die, but you are the future. The flag we have raised from nothing, we shall hand on to you, flesh of our flesh. Follow us everywhere. Before us, around us, behind us is Germany.' The beats from massed HJ drums are synchronized with the cheers.

As the fortunes of war moved against Germany the HJ took on a greater role in the defense of the Reich. The most famous element of the HJ was the 12 SS-Panzer-Division 'Hitlerjugend.' Formed in 1943 when Germany was becoming increasingly stretched in its search for manpower, the 12 SS-Panzer-Division had an average age of 18, though all its members had already built up a foundation of military skills in the HJ. It went into action on June 6 1944 against the Allied forces landing in Normandy. Though it fought with fanatical courage against British and Canadian troops,

Landdienst der HJ

GAU VERDEN

GAU THÜRINGEN

it was guilty of the murder of unarmed prisoners of war. It was all but destroyed in the savage fighting in Normandy. Refitted and reinforced it was used in the Ardennes Offensive of 1944-45 against US troops in Belgium. It was then switched to Hungary and Austria where it fought a hopeless action against the massive Soviet advance. At the close of the war only 455 men and one tank remained out of a division which, at its peak in December 1944, stood at 23,244. The survivors managed to extricate themselves from contact with the Russians and, less than a mile from the US lines, SS-Brigadeführer und Generalmajor der Waffen-SS Hugo Krass inspected the remains of his division in one last parade before they surrendered to the Americans.

Members of the HJ who had not volunteered for the Waffen SS or passed through the ranks of the HJ and entered the armed forces, were pressed into duties in the defense of the Reich as the Allied air offensive increased. Young women and youths became flak crews or part of the fire and rescue services.

At the age of 19 or 20, young Germans could join the NSDAP or Nazi Party which entitled them to wear a Party badge in their lapels. With a swastika at the center, it was a circular badge with a wreath surrounding an inner band with the words *National Sozialistische DAP*. The first 100,000 members of the NSDAP were entitled to wear the *Goldenes Parteiabzeichen*, the golden party badge. The lower the number, the closer the owner was to Hitler's circle (he had badge number 7). The golden badge came in two sizes – large for uniforms and a smaller size for civilian clothes. A member's number also gave an indication whether he had joined before or after the Nazis came to power. A low party number was an indication that an individual was a true Nazi, while a high one suggested that he or she had joined out of self interest. Numbers, however, could be flexible, and late, but favored arrivals could receive a low number. Other privileged Party members wore the *Blutorden*, a medal originated in 1933 which was issued to the 1500 Nazis who took part in the

ABOVE: The Führer signs autographs for young HJ members and a 'civilian' boy in lederhosen.

LEFT: Hitler Youth with Kar98k rifles on a range at an annual camp. M43 caps and uniforms show that this is late in the war.

BELOW: The NSDAP party badge. There were two versions, a larger one for wear on uniforms and a smaller for civilian jackets. Party membership gave access to benefits and privileges, but also carried responsibility within the community. Within the SS, 'Old Fighters', who had been members of the party before it came to power, wore distinctive arm chevrons, the SS-Armwinkel.

ABOVE: A collection of political badges which includes (1) *Stahlhelm*, a nationalist ex-servicemen's organization established in 1918; (2) NSBO, *Nationalsozialistische Betriebsorganisation*, the precursor of the DAF; (3) DJV, *Deutsches Jungvolk*, the junior section of the HJ; (4) NSF, *Nationalsozialist-Frauenschaft*, the women's organization; (5) NSFK, *Nationalsozialistisches Fliegerkorps*, the flying organization; (6) NSLB, *NS-Lehrerbund*, the Teachers' Alliance; (7) the badge of a Nazi Christian association; (8) a small Party Badge.

LEFT: Fifty National Socialists marry in a mass wedding at the Lazarkirche in Berlin in 1936. A senior member of the SA wearing his decorations from World War I heads the 'parade'. The senior SA groom looks mildly worried and behind him is another, who despite his dark uniform is not a member of the SS , but one of the many NSDAP organizations.

Munich *putsch* on November 9, 1923. Each medal was numbered and was made from silver with a red ribbon with white enclosure. Long serving Party members could also qualify for the *Dienstauszeichnungen der NSDAP*, the Long Service Award of the NSDAP. This was a Maltese cross-style decoration which came in three classes, bronze for ten years, blue enamel for 15 years and white enamel for 25 years. On the reverse were the words *Treue für Führer und Volk* – 'Loyalty to Leader and People.'

The Nazi Party penetrated the whole of German society and was organized in an elaborate pyramidic structure with Hitler at the apex as Führer, Chancellor, and leader of the Reich. The Reich leadership was formed by 17 *Reichsleitern*, or ministers, who held portfolios for finance, justice, armaments and war production, and propaganda, among others. Each *Reichsleiter* was responsible directly to Hitler. The Party was structured so that Nazi policy could be carried out at the low-

TOP LEFT: Young and old members of the SA in the Classless Society – *Volksgemeinschaft*.

ABOVE: Cuff title and badge for the *NS-Frauenschaft*, NS Women's Groups.

LEFT: Hitler and Albert Speer (left foreground) inspect a new German tank. In the background are officers of the army, Waffen-SS and mountain troops. Close combat badges, the Russian winter campaign 1941-42 medal and the German Cross worn by officers show that it is probably in 1943.

ABOVE RIGHT: The SA 'Brown Shirt' seen here with Sports Badge and armband. The shirt was well made from a gabardine material.

FAR RIGHT: A *Gau*-level NSDAP leader's shirt. It has a World War I EK1 and Wound Badge.

est levels: *Gaue* (regions), *Kreise* (districts), *Ortsgruppen* (groups), *Zellen* (street cells), and *Blocke* (blocks). There were ten *Landesinspekteure*, nine in Germany and one in Austria; similarly there were 32 *Gaue* in Germany proper and ten in the annexed territories. The *Landesinspekteure* reported to the *Reichsleitern* and were responsible for four *Gaue*. Beneath the *Gaueleiters* was an army of lesser officials: the *Kreisleiter*, or district leaders; the *Ortsgruppenleiter*, or local group leaders; the *Zellenleiter*, or cell leaders responsible for a neighborhood or employment unit; finally the *Blockwart*, the block warden responsible for a couple of households. Individual Party members were known as *Parteignosse*, party comrade, or PG for short. In an ideal world this structure meant that the elderly and sick were not neglected and the fabric of society remained strong. Unfortunately it also allowed petty officials to snoop and intrude, and the internal security system to impose a high level of control.

Officers and functionaries of the NSDAP wore a brown uniform with a swastika arm band. The cap had a darker brown band and gold cord chin strap and trim. The belt was brown leather. Rank was displayed on collar patches; if the wearer was a service leader, in undress uniform he would wear a double-breasted jacket and black trousers – a style favored by Hitler.

As we observed in the introduction, the SS had their own distinctive black uniform. They provided the body

guards in major public buildings and guards of honor for visiting VIPs. The regular army called the SS 'asphalt soldiers' since they were originally only parade ground soldiers; as the war developed and the Waffen-SS were used as tough 'firemen' to plug gaps on the front or lead attacks, the army respected their fighting prowess. They received the full range of gallantry decorations during the war, but also had their own unique medals. The SS *Dienstauszeichnungen*, Long Service Award came in four classes – black for four years, bronze for eight, a silver swastika design with SS runes on the ribbon for 12 years and a gilt swastika of similar design for 25 years.

In many ways the early Nazi Party seemed to be embodied by the 'Storm Troopers' of the SA *Sturmabteilung*. The name was derived from the First World War raiding parties which had been assembled to attack Allied trench lines. The SA earned the nickname 'Brown Shirts' from the early uniform which was in a color then uncharacteristic in Germany. It was a mustard khaki and consisted of a shirt, breeches and marching boots. Headgear was a képi-style cap, the crown and the collar patches were in a shade of cerise. Leather equipment was brown. The SA dagger had a dark brown wooden hilt with eagle and swastika and a brown metal scabbard. The blade had the motto ALLES FÜR DEUTSCHLAND – 'All for Germany.' The SA who had served in the First World War wore their decorations, but there

LEFT: Reichsführer Himmler at Dachau KZ (Konzentrations Lager) on a visit in May 1936. He wears the 9 November *Blutorden* (Blood Order) on his right breast pocket.

BELOW LEFT: The four-pocket uniform of an *Ortsgruppenleiter* (Local Branch Leader) 1936-38 (3rd pattern). Above the EK1 is an old Party campaign badge. The tunic is made from good quality gabardine and is in a brown shade similar to a military uniform.

BELOW: The fourth pattern uniform for a *Haupt-Gemeinschaftsleiter Ortsgruppe* 1939-45. The buttons are now dull mid-brown unlike prewar buttons which were gilt and bore a small 'political' eagle. The belt is gold brocade on velvet. The cap has the light blue piping of the *Ortsgruppe*.

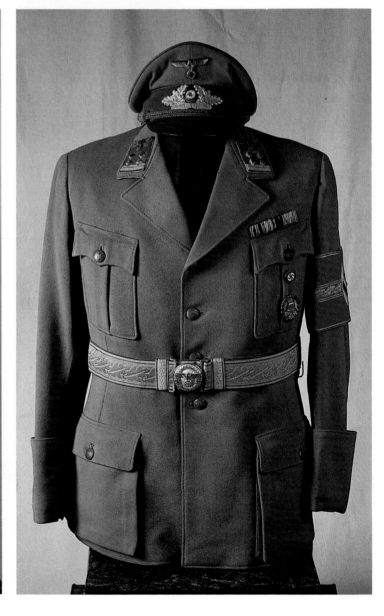

ABOVE: SA sports badges which would have been sewn on to singlets and track suits.

ABOVE LEFT: SA cuff title, armband, epaulet and collar patch. The pink color to the patch and black numbers suggests that the insignia is from Gruppe Ostmark. Insignia changed as the SA took on new tasks and the Reich expanded with the war.

LEFT: Berlin SA men burn a red, black and gold flag in March 1933. It is probably a banner taken from the Communist HQ in the city. Flags, uniforms and insignia were important to the Communists and nationalist movements in Europe in the 1920s and '30s.

TOP LEFT: SA cap of a subaltern of Gruppe Pomerania with green top, black/white piping, gold button and the silver 1929-34 cap badge.

ABOVE: An early NSDAP officer's cap; it is distinguishable by its silver piping and silver cord chin strap.

LEFT: A *Reichsleiter's* summer-pattern cap – the design and style of the eagle (national emblem) show that this is a later pattern cap. *Reichsleiteren* were heads of the departments and executives of the NSDAP.

BOTTOM: A wartime *Gauleiter's* cap. The *Gauleiter* were appointed by Hitler and answered to him.

TOP RIGHT: The far hat is a *Kreisleiter's* white piped visored cap. A *Kreis* (circuit) was a county or region and was the main subdivision of a *Gau*. The M43 cap (near hat) with its BeVo – quality badge is for members of an *Ordensburg* (Order Castle). The four *Ordensburgen* were training centers for future Nazi leaders.

RIGHT: An *Ostministerium* officer's cap with a large 'political' eagle. The brown-gold color of the uniforms of members of the Ostministry earned them the pejorative nickname from front line soldiers 'golden pheasants'.

was also the SA *Wehrabzeichen*, the SA Military Sports Badge, which consisted of a Roman sword against a swastika surrounded by an oak wreath. It was awarded in bronze, silver and gilt and there was a special award for the wounded in bronze. Interestingly this badge paralleled an older institution, the *Deutsches Reichsabzeichen für Leibesübungen*, the German National Badge for Physical Training. This had the letters DRL enclosed within a wreath and was awarded in bronze, silver and gilt. After the Nazis came to power the badge received a swastika at its base. As the war developed the SA were pressed into service, and though there were official uniforms in an earth gray with an M1943 cap, it

was more common for men to wear the standard Wehrmacht field gray.

At the age of 19 or 20 men were called up for labor and military service. In an ideal career the men would toughen up during their six months of labor service with the *Reichsarbeitsdienst* (RAD), and then be conscripted into the armed forces. The RAD was introduced by the law of June 26 1935 which affected men and women between the ages of 19 and 25. Men worked on agricultural and public works including building defenses and air-raid shelters. Women were later incorporated into the system and were required to undertake domestic service and traditional female agricultural

FAR LEFT: SA sports badges in bronze and gold. A special version was produced for wounded SA athletes.

LEFT: Viktor Lutze, Chief of Staff of the SA, who took over after Röhm's murder. He has gold long service cuff bands and decorations from his service as an officer in World War I.

BELOW LEFT: A *Luftschutze* (air raid precautions) gladiator-style helmet painted in SA colors and with the SA decal on the side.

RIGHT: *Reichsarbeitsdienst* (RAD) badges showing the spade and wheat ear motif. On the right is a strip of badges which have not been embroidered with unit numbers.

BELOW RIGHT: RAD men in parade uniforms – the striking ski cap style can be seen.

tasks. The first annual contingents numbered 200,000 men organized into two units. The introduction of the RAD had the immediate effect of reducing unemployment which made Hitler more popular.

The RAD also appear in the film *Triumph of the Will*. With spades shouldered like rifles they chant like a Greek chorus, 'We stand here. We are ready.' There is a roll-call of the *Gau* represented. The chant resumes with 'Ein Volk, Ein Reich, Ein Führer. We plant trees. We build streets. We give the farmers new acres. For Germany.' The chant of 'Ein Volk, Ein Reich, Ein Führer' (One People, One Reich, One Leader), like 'Sieg Heil,' (Hail Victory) was a feature of Nazi rallies and like any mass shouting, had a way of hypnotizing the participating audience. 'Sieg Heil' was also a Party greeting and became a battle cry for German soldiers on the attack.

In the sequence in *Triumph of the Will* featuring the RAD at Nuremberg, slow music follows the chorus chant and the flags are ceremonially lowered. The spades are shouldered beneath the skeleton of the *Reichsadler* mounted above the Nuremberg Stadium. Hitler watches with 'grimly benevolent concentration' then he addresses them: 'Earth and labor unite us all. The entire nation goes through your school. Germany is happy to see her sons marching.'

The uniform and insignia of the RAD was stylish and imaginative. It consisted of a khaki brown tunic and trousers with marching boots; in service dress men wore a ski cap with insignia of a spade flanked by ears of wheat on the front. In working order the cap was re-

placed by a side cap. Women wore a jacket and long skirt with a rather shapeless hat. The spade insignia also appeared on the left sleeve with the blade pointing down bearing the RAD unit number. A standard swastika arm band was worn. Rank was displayed on the jacket collars and reflected the nature of the RAD's work using motifs like ears of wheat and the shovel. As with other organizations within the Nazi Party, the RAD had an edged weapon. In keeping with its workmanlike role this was a broad-bladed hewer with a horn grip and the motto ARBEIT ADELT (Work Enobles) on the blade.

The RAD instituted Long Service Awards of the National Labor Service, *Dienstauszeichnungen für den Reichsarbeitsdienst*. They were in four classes with different configurations for men and women. The women's was worn as a brooch hanging from a bow and featured a swastika supported by two ears of wheat, while the men's was a medal with the shovel and wheat motif.

Ein Volk, ein Reich, ein Führer!

The awards were for four years, 12 years, 18 years and 25 years – which, given the lifespan of the Thousand Year Reich, presumably means that only the bronze four year awards were distributed. The other classes of decoration were made from silver, silver with a silver eagle on the ribbon, and gilt metal with a gilt eagle.

The rest of the RAD uniform consisted of a mustard khaki shirt with a black tie. Belts and other fittings were in black leather and the paramilitary style that had begun with the HJ was continued with men carrying packs, water bottles and mess tins. In part this military style made sense, since men would be deployed on construction tasks in rural areas and would need to be reasonably self-sufficient.

Instead of serving in the RAD a young man (women were encouraged in more 'womanly pursuits') could join the Nazi Party and either enter the SA, SS or the NSKK (*Nationalsozialistische Kraftfahrkorps*) and NSFK (*Nationalsozialistische Fliegerkorps*). The NSKK had been set up initially in 1931 to give the SA transportation and trained drivers. It survived the Night of the Long Knives and after 1933 concentrated on training drivers for the armed forces. As a branch of the Party the NSKK had its own regional organization which was divided into *Motorobergruppen* and further into *Motorgruppen*. With the outbreak of war the NSKK had three tasks. It organized pre-military training in the motorized branch of the Hitler Youth, provided auxiliary transportation in the communications zone in support of the armed forces, and trained tank crews for the army. At the close of the war the NSKK became responsible for training members of the *Volkssturm*, the Home Guard formed in 1944.

Initially the NSKK wore a khaki tunic and black breeches with a mustard khaki shirt and black tie. Its connection with the SA was emphasized by the SA-style képi which had a black top and khaki sides. A black diamond on the lower left sleeve had a white wheel motif and above it was the almost obligatory swastika arm band. Rank was displayed on the collar, and a black leather Sam Browne belt was worn by officers. A ribbed black leather crash helmet was worn by drivers and motorcyclists. The NSKK wore the SA dagger, but it had a brown grip and black metal scabbard.

With the onset of war the NSKK rationalized its uniform and men wore a khaki tunic with a brown collar, a color which was repeated in the cap band. Rank was displayed on the closed stand-and-fall collar. A distinctive NSKK eagle and swastika (the national emblem) appeared on the cap and on the upper left sleeve and consisted of an eagle, swastika and wreath with a scroll behind the wings with the letters NSKK. This insignia was repeated on the belt buckles of officers and enlisted men. They also wore the NSKK diamond on the lower sleeve. As the war developed the NSKK formed Air

LEFT: One of the classic poster images of the Führer, Adolf Hitler, with the slogan 'One People, One State, One Leader!' Slogans like this were chanted at rallies and could reduce audiences to an almost trance-like state. The poster also gives some idea of the hypnotic power of Hitler's intense eyes.

BELOW LEFT: The NSKK, *Nationalsozialistiches Kraftfahr-Korps* (the Nazi transport corps) which operated vehicles, trained tank crews and, as the cuff title indicates, was also involved in air transportation. They were the only overtly Nazi organization to be part of the *Deutsches Afrika Korps* (DAK) where they serviced and operated vehicles in North Africa between 1941 and 1943.

RIGHT: A tank crewman, NSKK man, and Hitler Youth step boldly into an unforeseen future in this Nazi propaganda poster. The route from youth, through the NSKK, to service as a tank soldier, was a logical progression for German males. The Panzerwaffe (tank arm) was an elite within the army and Waffen-SS.

LEFT: The NSKK crash helmet with characteristic eagle.

BELOW LEFT: NSKK motoring plaques from the 1930s. They record rallies undertaken by the driver and vehicle breakdown services. The Nazis were quick to realize that driving, flying and parachuting were skills of the future and they sponsored and promoted them to enhance the image of a new nation.

TOP RIGHT: An NSKK car pennant.

RIGHT: Glider proficiency badges – third class with one seagull, second with two and first with three. Gliding, while exciting, was also a way of introducing German youth to basic flying skills which was the first step to training pilots for the Luftwaffe. The NSRL Physical Training League badges below also reflect the emphasis on fitness which meant that German soldiers were capable of marching huge distances on the Eastern Front.

Transport Regiments which handled the movement of men and equipment. Men in these regiments wore uniforms in the color and cut of the Luftwaffe, but had black side hats with the NSKK eagle on the left, as well as the sleeve which also displayed the diamond. On the cuff was the title with the number and words 'NSKK Transport Regiment'.

The *Nationalsozialistische Fliegerkorps* (NSFK) came into existence in April 1937 when the Nazi government incorporated existing aviation clubs and associations into one body. Its mission became to train potential pilots for the Luftwaffe, post-military training of reservists and to further air-mindedness amongst the German population. Its greatest success before the war was with glider training for the HJ. Simple winch-launched gliders gave youthful pilots their first experience of flight and produced a powerful propaganda image of a new nation taking to the skies.

As with every other organization within Nazi Germany the NSFK had a uniform. Service dress was in

Luftwaffe gray, with a pale blue shirt and black tie. An SA-style képi in the same color was piped with yellow – the *Waffenfarbe* (arm color) of aircrew and paratroopers in the Luftwaffe. The right sleeve had a striking motif which was a winged man in white with a pale blue border above a black swastika. Collars had rank and unit details. The summer uniform had a mustard khaki shirt, black tie, swastika armband, and rank on the collar on a Luftwaffe gray background. Trousers were gray, and belts and fittings in black leather. The NSFK instituted awards for powered, balloon and glider flight. Powered was initially a wreathed eagle, but this was replaced by a badge with a symbolic aircraft and a small version of the NSFK winged man. Balloon flight also

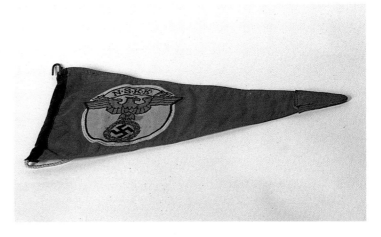

Hilf siegen
als Luftnachrichtenhelferin

went through changes, beginning as a badge in which the balloon was the dominant image; the later version reduces the balloon and has instead more emphasis on the winged swastika and oak wreath. The glider pilot's badge did not change and is an elegant design with three seagulls wreathed above the NSFK insignia.

Between the ages of 21 and 23 the youthful citizen of Nazi Germany would fulfil his military service. However, as the war progressed this two year period became as long as five years and men who had served in the 1930s were recalled.

Following his time in the military a man might enter government service or industry. Even here the Nazi state had uniforms, insignia and the outward trappings of power. There was even insignia for the *Nationalsozialistsche Betriebszellenorganisation*, the National Socialist Shop Cell Organization, which replaced the propaganda function of older trades unions in factories and plants. According to a contemporary joke the letters NSBO actually stood for 'Noch sind die Bozen oben' – 'The party favorites are still on top.' NSBO had a motif which featured a hand holding a hammer which had a swastika against a cog wheel design bearing the letters NSBO, the whole design being surrounded by a wreath.

However, it was the *Deutsche Arbeitsfront* (DAF), the German Labor Front which had the greatest impact in the work place. DAF members could wear a black uniform with side cap – pale blue piping edged the epaulets and cap. The DAF belt buckle featured a swastika within a cog wheel, while leaders had this design within a wreath. The DAF was a vast organization with a nominal membership of 20 million. Its function for the Nazi government was to create conditions in the work-place in which industrial discord and strikes would disappear. Paid holidays and sports facilities were organized through the *Kraft durch Freude* (KdF), the 'Strength through Joy' movement. The Volkswagen or 'People's Car' was a product of the KdF movement and workers could pay weekly instalments towards its purchase. It was not produced in large numbers, however, as the factory soon had to change to military vehicle production.

The KdF movement was seen as an attempt to introduce a classless, hardworking community to a reborn Germany. Most civil uniforms were based around a tunic with breeches and boots, or long trousers and shoes, with a peaked officers' or NCO-style cap. Some tunics, like those for the Diplomatic Corps, Water Protection Police or the Order Police (*Ordnungspolizei* or ORPO) were double-breasted. The ORPO Mountain Gendarmerie, however, had a ski cap with Eidelweiss insignia similar to army and Waffen-SS mountain troops. A common feature of the Order Police insignia was a *Wehrmachtadler* enclosed by a wreath. This was worn on the left sleeve and as a cap badge. The design was also incorporated into the grip of the bayonet-style sidearm carried by police. This had an eagle's head as the pommel, with horn grips and chromed blade. The Police Protection Service, (*Schutzpolizei*) had a blue-gray tunic with earthbrown collar and cuffs, and green trousers. Collar patches for several branches of the Order Police were similar to those of the army; tunics, trousers, epaulets and caps were piped with branch colors *(Truppenfarbe)* to show the area of service. The ORPO *Wasserschutzpolizei*, (Water Police) had a navy

FAR LEFT: A blonde and smiling Luftwaffe air defense auxiliary with Flak *Waffenfarbe* piping on her side hat.

LEFT: The *Reichs Luftschutzbund* (RLB) or Reich Air Defense League breast badge, collar patches and shoulder strap of an officer. RLB officers also wore a special dress dagger.

BELOW LEFT: A *Deutsche Arbeitsfront* (DAF) *Gauwerksscharführer* – German Labour Front Gau Works leader uniform. The DAF swastika and cogwheel insignia appears on shoulder straps, tie pin and on some belt buckles.

RIGHT: The *Nationalsozialistiches Fliegerkorps* (NSFK) epaulets, collar patches and breast badge. The NSFK 'winged man' was a striking image for an organization intended to foster air-mindedness. The NSFK grew out of the older *Deutsche Luftsports Verein* (DLV).

LEFT: Backed by an HJ band and choir and the *Deutsche Arbeitsfront* symbol, Hitler launches the 'People's Car', the Volkswagen, on May 26 1938. The VW 'Beetle' lasted longer than the Thousand Year Reich which spawned it. The Volkswagen was one of the KDF projects which allowed workers to buy a car by purchasing a large quantity of saving stamps over a long period of time.

RIGHT: Police insignia. (1-3) Fire Protection, Gendarmerie and Water Protection Police arm badges; (4-5) epaulets for a Schupo Wachtmeister and Meister of Gendarmerie; (6) a *Schutzpolizei* sports vest badge.

BELOW: Hitler in his 'uniform' — a neutral double-breasted blazer with gold military-style buttons. He had an army-style national emblem on the left sleeve in the SS manner. His Iron Cross First Class could be added if the situation dictated.

blue uniform with gold-colored buttons, white shirt, black tie and gold-colored rank insignia. The Water Police patrolled docks and waterways in speed boats, and officers had an elegant naval-style dagger with an anchor motif on the guard. The *Luftshutzpolizei* (Air Protection Police) had a field-gray uniform with slate-gray piping, though the cap had a black band.

A close ally of this force were the *Technische Nothilfe* or TeNo, the voluntary Technical Emergency Service who had originally provided the manpower and expertise for industrial and building projects, and were later tasked with air raid clearance. TeNo became the heros of the airwar against the Reich, and their dark gray uniforms featured a distinctive sleeve eagle with a swastika and a cog wheel enclosing a sledge hammer making a 'T' with the letter 'N'. TeNo officers wore a buckle with the TeNo-style National Symbol surrounded by a laurel wreath. Reflecting their tough role, TeNo had a broad-bladed hewer. The TeNo officers' dagger was an elegant double-edged weapon bearing the TeNo eagle as a guard. Though there were specifically TeNo awards, as the war developed they would also have qualified for medals like the *Luftschutz Ehrenzeichen*, (Civil Defense Decoration) which came in two classes, or the *Rettungsmedaille* (Life Saving Medal).

The *Schutzpolizei* in Prussia, which was the largest police force in Germany when the Nazis came to power, had a belt buckle with an eagle with its back visible; officers had the words FREISTAAT PREUSSEN around the

TOP LEFT: A Police M43 cap – the red, black and white national cockade is interestingly above the police national emblem.

ABOVE: A Police Administration officer's cap, very similar in design to a standard military cap.

LEFT: A *Deutsche Reichsbahn* (railway) inspector's cap with its characteristic winged wheel and striking red and Prussian blue colors.

BELOW LEFT: A TeNo officer's cap, TeNo – *Technische Nothilfe* was a voluntary organization which provided manpower and expertise for industrial and building projects. The hewer, which was part of the uniform, had a cog wheel device on the pommel and the cross guard had an eagle grasping a cog wheel and swastika.

LEFT: The striking German police shako – this one is for rural police. Germany had several police forces including the ORPO – *Ordnungspolizei* (Order Police), and the SIPO – *Sicherheitspolizei* (Security Police) which was composed of the Gestapo – *Geheime Staatspolizei* (Secret State Police) and the *Kriminalpolizei* – KRIPO (Criminal Police).

BELOW: An armband for the *Organization Todt* (OT), with speciality badges for bricklayer and carpenter. The OT was a semi-military governmental construction unit set up in 1938. It built motorways and most of the massive concrete defensive lines in Occupied France and on the German border, as well as bunkers and air raid shelters. It was administered by Dr Fritz Todt until his death in 1942, when Albert Speer took over.

edge of the buckle, while police had a laurel wreath. The *Schupo*, the ordinary urban constabulary, had a buckle with a swastika at the center and the motto GOTT MIT UNS – God with us. The *Landespolizei* who policed the 15 *lander* or states which made up the Third Reich had a buckle with the wreathed *Wehrmachtadler*. The police had a range of decorations for long service, or *Polizei dienstauszeichnungen*: a silver medal for eight years, a silver cross for 18 years and a gilt cross for 25 years. Both medal and cross had the characteristic police eagle and wreath as central motifs.

In a world in which everyone was in uniform, the man or woman in civilian clothes was suspected as a slacker. Eventually even the Diplomatic Corps and government officials wore uniforms of dark blue-black, with a brown leather Sam Browne belt and a cap with an extravagant diplomatic National Emblem (this bird had oversized wings which spread across the cap). It may seem unlikely, but swords and daggers were even produced for the prison and judicial service. They had no obvious symbols on their blade, guard or grip, but reflect the Nazi German concern to wear uniforms which approximated to those worn by the military.

The Diplomatic Corps had a uniform similar to that of the government officials, though without the Sam Browne belt, and with gold-colored buttons. Rank was displayed both on the cuffs and the epaulets and the insignia on the cap was also gold-colored. Swords and daggers were also part of the uniform – daggers had the attraction that they could be worn as part of dress wear, but were less cumbersome than swords. Both edged weapons had a stylized eagle's head as the pommel.

LEFT: A TeNo arm band and cuff title. Though arm bands were worn as political trappings, they were also useful to identify men who were dressed in anonymous overalls who might be working clearing rubble on bombed sites.

BELOW: TeNo cuff titles. The cuff title in German military and paramilitary uniforms was either honorific or identified divisions or regiments. As battle honors, they had the same function as campaign ribbons, while with units they were similar to British cap badges or regimental shoulder titles or US Army patches.

BOTTOM: RAD unit cuff titles.

LEFT: Shoulder straps and RVD badge for the State Traffic Directorate. Interestingly, the badge is for the Ukrainian city of Dnjepropetrovsk, where the RVD would have operated the rail links. The *Reichsbahn* arm band would have been worn by laborers on the railways. The rubber stamp on the arm band could be verified by comparing it with that in the laborer's pass.

BELOW: Cuff titles for *Reichsbahn* officials working in Brussels and Paris. The railways in Occupied Europe were essential to move German forces and their tanks and artillery from the Eastern Front to Italy or to the coast where they manned defenses.

Customs officials were uniformed, as might be expected, and wore a gray-green uniform with darker green collar and cap band. They also featured a characteristically German feature, the cuff band. This was normally on the left sleeve about six to eight inches above the cuff. In the Customs uniform it bore a special National Emblem on a green background. The force had

its own dagger, based on the Model 1935 army dagger. The Nazi government rationalized a number of administrative organizations which had previously been run on a state basis, and the introduction of standardized uniform and equipment assisted this move towards uniformity. The Customs service also qualified for medals such as the *Zollgrenzschutz Ehrenzeichen* – which was

LEFT: *Reichsbahnschutz* (Railway Protection Service) epaulets, and *Reichspost* arm badge and collar patches. The *Reichsbahnschutz* dated back to the turn of the century, when rail and waterway links became important for emerging industrial powers in Europe, and special forces were created to protect goods in transit, as well as the fabric of the system. During the war there was the problem of looting in bombed areas and sabotage in Occupied countries.

BELOW LEFT: A TeNo NCO's cap. TeNo was invaluable after air raids on the Reich when they deployed and operated heavy lifting equipment to assist in recovering surviving casualties.

BELOW: The massed ranks of the SA and SS in a prewar rally.

LEFT: Women's organizations' cuff titles. From the top the *Bund Deutscher Madel* (BDM) German Girls' League from Osteinsatz (1); a woman's work group (2); two army Staff Woman Assistants (literally 'helper') (3 & 4); and a Navy Woman Assistant title (5).

BELOW LEFT: Albert Speer (right) talks to a Luftwaffe officer who wears the Knight's Cross with Oak Leaves, as well as the German Cross, Wound Badge and Iron Cross First Class. Speer wears the Organization Todt arm band.

BELOW: A pass issued to SS-Oberscharführer Willi Haupt permitting him to travel in Paris from March to October 1944. It bears the inevitable eagle and swastika rubber stamp and the holder's paybook number.

awarded for four years service by uniformed staff and eight years by civilians.

The Reich railway service had a Prussian blue tunic and cap, and black trousers; trim on the cap and down the seam of the trousers was in red. This eye-catching uniform survived with obvious modifications after the war. The belt buckle had a winged wheel above a swastika surrounded by a wreath with the words DEUTSCHE REICHSBAHN. In 1938 a special protection unit for the Reich railways and waterways was established. Its function was to protect rolling stock and harbors. The *Reichsbahnschutz* had its own dagger which featured the winged wheel on the guard.

The mines, both nationally and privately owned, had accoutrements and medals. There were two classes of *Grubenwehr-Ehrenzeichen* (Mine Rescue Service Decoration), a pin-back and a ribbon version. They both featured a conventional *Reichsadler* backed by crossed miner's picks and hammer. The insignia of the National Bureau of Mines had an eagle holding a sword in one claw and a shield and lightning bolts in the other. On the shield are a crossed pick and hammer.

Even organizations as innocent as the postal service had quasi-police forces. The *Reich Postschutz* (Postal Protection Service) was tasked with the protection of the internal mail and communications of the Reich. They wore a slate gray uniform with dark gray cuff and collar; collar patches and trim were in scarlet with a distinctive scarlet *Wehrmachtadler* holding four lightning bolts and bugle horn on the left sleeve. Members of the *Postschutz* had their own dagger with a swastika on the guard and the *Postschutz* eagle on the grip. The belt buckle for both officers and men bore the word POSTSCHUTZ with the eagle, lightning bolts and horn.

ABOVE: A German postwoman effectively in civilian clothes; her cap and armband constitute a 'uniform'.

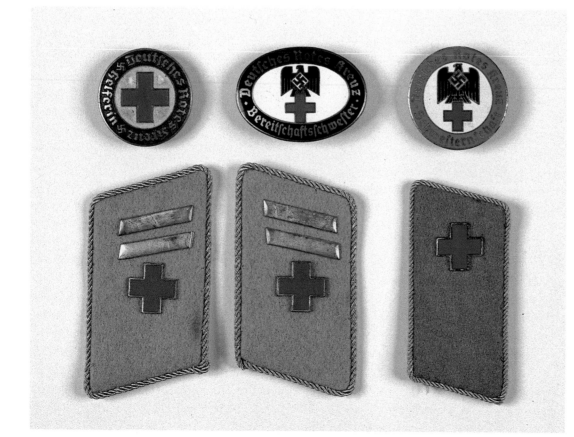

LEFT: German Red Cross collar patches and brooches for nursing. Red Cross members also had a blunt-ended, but saw-toothed hewer for making splints.

ABOVE RIGHT: The *Deutsche Jägerschaft* (German Hunting Association) epaulet and sleeve badge – a swastika replaces the old Christian cross in the antlers. Members also wore traditional short hunting swords as part of their uniform.

ABOVE FAR RIGHT: Army stretcher bearer's arm band worn on the right, and the arm band for civilian personnel attached to the army, worn on the left arm.

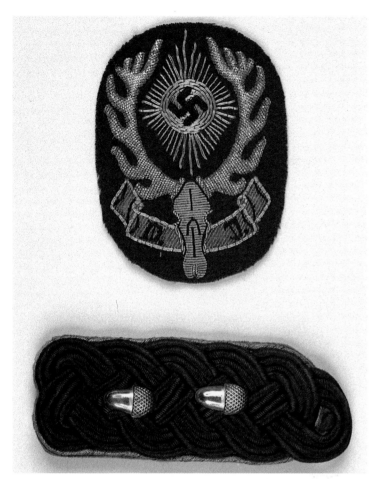

The German Red Cross did not escape the Nazification process. They wore a dark gray uniform with a pale gray cap band and collar patches. The patches had a red cross. The inevitable eagle and swastika were present – on the cap a black eagle held a red cross in its claws with a swastika on its breast, and this also appeared on the belt buckle. Equipment was in black leather and members of the Red Cross had a distinctive broad-bladed hewer. Since their function was to save life and relieve suffering, the hewer did not have a sharp point like a conventional weapon, but rather a 'chiselled' or 'square' tip. It did, however, have a saw blade on one side to allow members to cut through wood to construct splints. Officers had a more conventional dagger. The German Red Cross had its own range of decorations for men and women. The main feature of these medals was the *Reichsadler* at the center of a red cross. They ranged from the Decoration of the Red Cross which was worn on a ribbon, through the Cross of Merit, a First Class version of which was a neck order, a pin backed star, a Ladies' Cross, the *Damenkreuz* worn from a bow, and also a Women's Cross, *Frauenkreuz*, which one assumes was for junior-ranked female members of the Red Cross.

The intrusion into German private and domestic life by the Nazi government was almost boundless. Hunting, forestry and shooting clubs and organizations were absorbed and given new trappings. Göring, who enjoyed hunting, gave himself the title *Reichsjägermeister* (Reich Master Hunter) and it gave him the opportunity to sport several designs of hunting knife as well as dashing outfits. The numerous hunting organizations in Germany were incorporated into the *Deutsche Jäger-*

schaft in 1936 and with this they were obliged to adopt a standardized uniform. The traditional hunter's emblem which had featured a stag with a Christian cross between its antlers was replaced by a stag with a swastika in place of the cross. This design also appeared on the hunting cutlass, an edged weapon which originally had a defensive function when the hunter was a gamekeeper.

While civilian life was being subjected to increasing militarization, the government did not neglect the armed forces. The easy prewar victories over the Rhineland, Austria and Czechoslovakia were suitably commemorated. Civilians, as well as servicemen, who participated in the invasion of Austria, Czechoslovakia and Memel, received morale-boosting awards.

The Austrian Anschluss medal was finished in matt silver and had a red ribbon with black and white outer edges. The *Medaille zur Erinnerung an der 13 Marz 1938*, (Commemorative Medal of 13 March 1938) showed two figures representing ethnic Germans breaking the chains of Austrian bondage carrying the banner of National Socialism. The reverse had the wording EIN VOLK, EIN REICH, EIN FÜHRER around the edge and the words '13. MARZ 1938' in the center. A total of 318,689 were awarded.

When German servicemen invaded Czechoslovakia it was the second of the 'flower wars', as soldiers called these bloodless coups. The *Medaille zur Erinnerung an der 1. Oktober 1938* was similar to the Austrian Anschluss Medal but was in bronze, suspended from a ribbon with equal stripes of black, red and black with narrow white outer stripes. The medal was awarded to

ABOVE: A DDAC doctor's enamel plaque showing the staff of Aesculapius surmounting a *Reichsadler*.

LEFT: As the war swung against Germany the propaganda machine went into top gear. Here one of the sculptured *Reichsadler* which flanked the Nuremberg Stadium appears above the slogan – 'At the end stands victory!'

RIGHT: The *Reichskreigsflagge* (Reich War Flag) flutters above stylised warships in a poster exalting operations by the German Navy. The image draws on pictures of the Channel Dash on February 12, 1942 when the battlecruiser *Scharnhörst* and heavy cruiser *Prinz Eügen* made a run from the French port of Brest to Wilhelmshaven. Codenamed 'Operation Cerberus', it was a local triumph for the Luftwaffe and Kriegsmarine who outwitted the Royal Navy, RAF and coastal defenses in a daylight dash up the Channel. However, though the ships were safer from air attack in Germany they were no longer a threat to Allied shipping in the North Atlantic and so in the long term it was a defeat.

Am Ende steht der Sieg!

all persons who took part in the entry into the Sudetenland and was extended to those who had participated in the creation of the protectorate of Bohemia and Moravia. For soldiers who were involved in both operations a *Spange 'Prager Burg'*, the Prague Castle Bar was instituted.

The last of the 'flower wars' was the takeover of the district of Memel which had been ceded to Lithuania in 1924. Hitler demanded it and under pressure from both the USSR and Nazi Germany the country caved in. German troops occupied it on March 22 1939 and received the *Medaille zur Erinnerung an die Heimkehr des Memellandes*. The bronze medal was similar to the Austrian and Czech designs but with a ribbon in white, red and green which, ironically, were the colors of Lithuania.

COMBAT UNIFORMS, INSIGNIA & AWARDS

Spanish Interlude

The civil war in Spain, which began as a right-wing revolt in Spanish Morocco by Generals Mola and Franco in July 1936, saw the proxy involvement of both the Nazi and Fascist governments of Germany and Italy. Soviet forces backed the leftist Popular Front government.

The war has been described as the dress rehearsal for the Second World War since it allowed the external powers to operate aircraft, ships and weapons, and to rotate crews through Spain where they were able to gain operational experience. The unsung heroes, however, were the Luftwaffe, particularly the pilots of the 20 Ju52 transport aircraft who ferried Franco's Moroccan troops and men of the Spanish Foreign Legion from Tetuan to the aerodrome of Tablada at Seville. By the end of September 1936 they had moved 8899 soldiers, 44 field guns, 90 machine-guns and 137 tons of ammunition and equipment.

The Legion was reinforced between December 1936 and January 1937 with extra Luftwaffe personnel, aircraft, AA artillery and specialists from the army including two tank companies. Its total strength was about 20,000 men which compared to the 60,000 to 70,000 sent by the Italians to fight for the Nationalists. German warships, including the battleship *Deutschland* and U-boats *U33* and *U34* operating off the Spanish coast, assisted in interdicting supplies and shore bombardments.

The Legion had three commanders: Generalmajor Hugo Sperrle who returned to Germany in November 1937; Generalleutnant Helmut Volkmann, and

ABOVE: The Condor Legion parade through the Brandenburg Gate on June 6 1939, with Spanish and German flags fluttering above them. Officers in the front rank are wearing the *Spanienkreuz* (Spanish Cross).

LEFT: Full military honors at the funeral of casualties from the battleship *Deutschland*, 1937.

RIGHT: An M43 tunic with EK1, *Infanterie-Sturmabzeichen* (Infantry Assault Badge), *Nahkampfspange* (Close Combat bar), and the ribbon for the *Erinnerungs Medaille für die Spanischen Freiwilligen im Kampf gegen den Bolschewismus* (Commemorative Medal for Spanish Volunteers in the Battle against Communism) looped through the tunic button hole.

PREVIOUS PAGES: Soldiers in the Model 1916 helmet bearing the *Reichsadler* transfer.

Generalmajor Wolfram Freiherr von Richthofen who returned to Germany with the Condor Legion at the close of the war. Von Richthofen was a cousin of the First World War ace the 'Red Baron' and though not a fighter expert, his dive bombers in Fliegerkorps 8 were instrumental in the victories of 1939 – 1941.

The Condor Legion received plaudits from both the Spanish and German governments. From the Spanish they received an *Ehrenstandarte* (Honor Standard) which was paraded at Barajas in April 1939. It was carried at Madrid and at the final parade at Leon in Spain. In Germany it was used for the official reception at

Hamburg and the parade of honor in Berlin. It was captured by the Soviet Army at the close of the war and is now held in the Central Museum of the USSR Armed Forces.

The flag has a staff topped with the Luftwaffe eagle and the colors are in red and yellow – the colors of Nationalist Spain. Prominent features are a silveredged iron cross with the Luftwaffe eagle at the center on the left side; on the right are red and yellow bars with the arms of Spain in the center. The arms are a black eagle flanked by the pillars of Hercules representing Gibraltar and Ceuta; they have scrolls with the words

LEFT: Luftwaffe pilot with ribbon bar and German Cross, EK1 and Bomber Clasp.

BELOW: First World War and Spanish Civil War (bottom) Wound Badges.

RIGHT: The German medal for Spanish volunteers on the Eastern Front hung, incorrectly, on the 1941-42 Winter Campaign ribbon.

FAR RIGHT: France, 1940. Rommel wearing the *Pour le Mérite* and Knight's Cross, talks to an officer wearing the Condor Legion tank attack badge from the Spanish Civil War (right).

'Plus' and 'Ultra' derived from the phrase 'Non plus Ultra', 'There is nothing beyond,' from the ancient idea that the world ended beyond the pillars of Hercules. The eagle holds a yoke and a bundle of five arrows. The eagle and arrows also appear on the left side of the flag in the corners. The arrows are said either to represent the archers who saved Spain from the Moors or the five old Spanish kingdoms. The yoke either represents the yoke of the Moors or the amalgamation of the kingdoms of Aragon and Castilia. Behind the eagle's head is a scroll with the words 'Une Grande Libre' – 'One great, free nation.'

The men of the Condor Legion received decorations for their hard work. A pinback medal, the *Spanienkreuz* (Spanish Cross) was in the form of a Maltese Cross with a swastika on its point in two circles in the center of the cross. A Luftwaffe eagle was affixed between each of the four arms of the cross. Combatants had a version with crossed swords behind the cross, while non-combatants had one without swords.

There were six grades which were presented in the following numbers. Bronze with swords – 8462; bronze without swords – 7869; silver with swords – 8304; silver without swords – 327; gold with swords – 1126; gold with swords and diamonds – 27. The Spanish Cross in gold with diamonds was for extraordinary service and was awarded personally by Hitler. To receive the cross with swords a recipient had to be a volunteer in the Condor Legion or to have taken part in one of the following naval actions: the air attack directed against the battle-

ship *Deutschland* in the waters off Ibiza on May 29 1937; the reprisal bombing of Almeira on May 31 1937; or the bombing attacks on German ships off Palma in May 1937. Non-combatants were personnel who had served as courier pilots or were civilian technicians.

A smaller version of the Spanish Cross without swords and suspended from a 30mm ribbon was instituted by Hitler on April 14 1939 for the next-of-kin of fallen volunteers in Spain. Some 315 were awarded; when worn by a woman the ribbon could be made into a bow.

Oberst Ritter von Thoma who commanded all the German armored forces in Spain, instituted a tank battle badge in the autumn of 1936. Von Thoma subsequently fought in Poland, France, the Soviet Union and North Africa. The badge was white metal with the traditional skull-and-cross bones with a symbolic tank below it surrounded by an oak wreath. Only 415 tank battle badges were given. It was worn on the lower left breast, ranking below the Iron Cross First Class and other war badges.

A wound badge, based on the First World War design instituted in March 1918, was reintroduced for men wounded in the Spanish campaign. The 1936/39 wound badge was oval with the First World War pattern helmet with crossed swords behind it and a swastika on the helmet, surrounded by a laurel wreath. The black version was issued for two wounds, silver for three and four wounds and the gold for five or more. Only 182 black badges were issued and one silver.

Ade Polenland, Ade Frankreichland

By the late 1930s Nazi Germany presented Europe with an image of ruthless military efficiency which was only partly accurate. It had a modern air force and the navy was small, though it had a significant number of U-boats. The army had a large number of men under arms, but its armor and mechanized forces were not as great as outsiders imagined. Indeed, many of its soldiers marched or rode on horseback in the early years of the war and some were reliant on bicycles.

The German triumphs of 1939-40 were based on tactics which were entirely novel – the world was expecting a First World War-style slugging match with static defenses. The Germans used their conventional marching infantry to launch 'spoiling attacks' which drew the attention of the enemy high command, while simultaneously using their air power to destroy the enemy air force in the air and on the ground. The enemy, with no air reconnaissance, was now blind and confused by reports of attacks along a long front. At this juncture mechanized and armored forces were concentrated on a narrow front where dive bombers pounded the enemy positions. Armor and mechanized infantry punched through and drove deep into the rear of the enemy territory. Simultaneous thrusts along a front linked up to form pockets in which large numbers of enemy troops were trapped.

The first example of these tactics took place in Poland in September 1939. A startled world watched as an 'outer encirclement' and an 'inner encirclement' carved the country up in about a month. Following the success of German arms against the allied French and British forces in May 1940, an Italian journalist described these tactics as 'lightning war'; the phrase was taken up by the Germans and *Blitzkrieg* was born.

The Propaganda Ministry was diligent in its efforts to foster an image of German might. Songs, films, books and magazines celebrated triumphs. One marching song composed late in 1940 simply said *Ade Polenland, Ade Frankreichland* – Goodbye Poland, Goodbye France. Other songs were composed, *Das Lied der Fall-*

LEFT: A fine example of Nazi heroic art, similar in style to Soviet, Japanese and even British and US paintings of the same era; it shows the three armed servies of the Second World War.

RIGHT: A PzKpfw IV driver and radio operator in summer-weight clothing. The rose pink *waffenfarbe* are visible on the epaulets of the driver, while the radio operator wears a black panzer side hat.

BELOW: An MG34 machine gun in its sustained fire role, with a crew from the Waffen-SS Polizei-Grenadier-Division. They have the SS eagle on their sleeves, but the police eagle on their helmets.

schirmjäger – The Paratrooper's Song; *Kameraden auf See* – Comrades of the Sea; and perhaps most famous, *Der Panzerlied* – The Tankcrew Song.

Uniforms of the forces were well-designed, sturdy and often stylish. The *Panzerwaffe* – the tank arm – wore a uniform and insignia which was intended to be practical yet also to convey the elite status of the force. The black double-breasted jacket with concealed buttons, and baggy full length trousers and short boots, were in a color which did not show oil stains and did not have external buttons to catch on fittings inside the tank. Initially soldiers wore a loose fitting beret *(schutzmütze)* which covered a rubber padded crash helmet. Beret and helmet disappeared after the 1940 campaign and during the rest of the war soldiers wore a *feldmütze* side hat. The shirt was gray with a black tie and officers wore gray doeskin gloves. The collar patches were the most eye-catching feature since they were a white metal death's head with a border of rose pink piping. Pink was the *Waffenfarbe* (arm color) of panzer units. The combination of a black uniform with death's head collar patches was dramatic and fearsome.

LEFT: An M43 tunic badged for a Schütze of Panzer Division Grossdeutschland. The epaulets are of gray wool with white infantry *Waffenfarben* with 'GD' cyphers slip over loops. The 'Grossdeutschland' cuff title is in field-gray wool. The tunic has a Wound Badge and the ribbon of the medal *Winterschlacht im Osten 1941/2* (Winter campaign in Russia 1941/2). This medal was also known as the 'Frozen Meat Medal' by soldiers, since one of the criteria for the award was suffering a frozen limb for which a wound badge was issued. The first winter in Russia was not only very severe, but the German army had planned for the campaign to be over by autumn and so were not dressed or equipped for winter war.

RIGHT: An excellent M34 tunic badged for a Feldwebel of the 21st Infantry Division. It has an EK1 and a black Wound Badge which was issued for one or two wounds. Subsequently a silver award was issued for three and four wounds and gold for five or more. Recipients had the award entered into their service records. Within the Reich there were 24 different manufacturers of the badge and so there are small variations in design and construction. The Wehrmacht belt buckle with its motto 'Gott Mit Uns' (God with us) is clear. The belt was constructed from tough hide and supported ammunition pouches, a water bottle, an entrenching tool, a bayonet and a bread bag.

LEFT: A tailored officer's tunic for a Hauptmann (Captain) of an infantry training regiment. The cap, which lacks a chin strap, is an 'Old Style' Field Service Cap, and has the National Emblem and *Reichskokade* machine-embroidered. The ribbons of the EK2 and 1941/2 Winter medal are looped through the tunic button hole with the EK1 on the front.

RIGHT TOP: An 'Old Style' Field Service Cap; interestingly the crown of the cap has been stiffened. The cap was officially meant to have been withdrawn in April 1942, but remained in service until the close of the war.

RIGHT: An 'Old Style' Field Service Cap with orange cavalry *Waffenfarbe* faded to yellow. However, the most interesting feature is the small metal badge showing the semi-official 'Windhund' Panzer Division emblem of the 116th Panzer Division.

BELOW RIGHT: The aluminum-thread *Gebirgsjäger* Edelweiss badge which was introduced for wear by mountain troops in May 1939. It is attached to a Bergmütze – the mountain troops' practical cap, which was later adapted as the 1943 *Einheitsfeldmütze* or General Issue Field Cap. The cap could be buttoned down to cover the wearer's neck and cheeks and this design was to appear after the war in the combat uniforms of several NATO armies.

Das Lied der Fallschirmjäger

Worte und Musik von Friedrich Schäfer

Rot scheint die Sonne, fertig gemacht,
wer weiß, ob sie morgen für uns auch noch lacht?
Werft an die Motoren, schiebt Vollgas hinein,
startet los, flieget an, heute geht es zum Feind!
In die Maschinen, in die Maschinen!

Kamerad, da gibt es kein Zurück,
fern im Westen
stehen dunkle Wolken,
komm mit und zage nicht, komm mit!

Donnern Motoren — Gedanken allein,
denkt jeder noch schnell an die Lieben daheim.
Dann kommt, kameraden, zum Sprung das Signal,
und wir schweben zum Feind, zünden dort das Fanal.
Schnell wird gelandet, schnell wird gelandet.

Klein unser Häuflein, wild unser Blut,
wir fürchten den Feind nicht und auch nicht den Tod.
Wir wissen nur eines, wenn Deutschland in Not,
zu kämpfen, zu siegen, zu sterben den Tod.
An die Gewehre, an die Gewehre.

TOP LEFT: A panzer soldier by a PzKpfw IV Ausf D, SdKfz 161 wearing the black *Sonderbekleidung der Deutschen Panzertruppen*, (Special Tank uniform) and early-pattern beret which covered a rubber crash helmet. Black was adopted because it would not show oil stains from engine and track lubricants.

ABOVE: A propaganda postcard with the words of the 'Paratrooper's Song'.

LEFT: The black panzer feldmütz, which replaced the beret, has rose pink panzer *Waffenfarbe*.

RIGHT: A PzKpfw IV Ausf B SdKfz 161 with commander in black panzer uniform. The death's head insignia was sometimes confused with that of the SS.

LEFT: A Waffen-SS Hauptsturmführer's panzer uniform with officer's belt, EK1, silver *Verwundeten-Abzeichen* 1939, (Wound Badge for three for four wounds, or major injury like loss of a limb or eyesight), and the *Panzerkampfabzeichen* (Tank Battle Badge) awarded to crews who had participated in three different armored attacks on three different days.

The field gray cap has panzer rose pink piping and the SS death's head. With no wire springing in the crown, it was comfortable and practical headgear.

RIGHT: Epaulets for a Panzer officer and NCO; a BeVo cockade, and collar patches; a standard bearer's armshield in black and rose pink; a strip of uncut national emblems.

BELOW RIGHT: An M37 tunic and cap for a Waffen-SS Rottenführer of SS Panzer Division Totenkopf. His rank is displayed both as collar bars and arm chevron. He has the *Infanterie-Sturmabzeichen* (Infantry Assault Badge) which was awarded for three infantry assaults, armed reconnaissance, hand-to-hand combat or restoration of the line on three days. It was initially made out of silver plate over bronze, but by the end of the war it was made from metal alloy.

BELOW FAR RIGHT: A Panzer Feldwebel with EK2. His black uniform was designed so that there were no exposed buttons which could snag inside a tank. The NCO wears the mouse-gray shirt and black tie. A reed-green denim uniform with a large pocket on the chest, was developed from the black uniform, for wear in the summer. The black uniform had one drawback in that it clearly identified the wearer as a tank soldier, so if men in black uniforms were seen in the frontline there was a good chance that they were undertaking a reconnaissance on foot prior to a tank attack.

Following the victories in Poland, Generaloberst von Brauchitsch, Oberbefehlshaber des Heeres, Commander-in-Chief of the army from 1938-41, instituted the *Panzerkampfabzeichen* – the Tank Battle Badge. Initially it was in silver only and was authorized for award to officers and men who participated as tank commanders, gunners, drivers or radio operators in at least three different armored assaults on three different days. From June 1 1940, a bronze version was introduced for members of Panzer-Grenadier regiments, as well as for medical personnel who rode into combat in an armored vehicle to tend to the wounded. The bronze award also extended to crews of armored cars.

The badge showed a PzKpfw III surrounded by an oak wreath and surmounted by the *Reichsadler*. After June 1943 the badge was modified to show the number of accumulated days in actual combat. The numbers were inset in a small rectangle at the base of the badge and went from 25, through 75 to 100. The 25 and 50 versions had a black tank with silver wreath and national emblem and were slightly larger than the standard badge. The 75 and 100 versions were larger still and were finished in gilt. For non-tank crews the badge for 25 and 50 was in bronze, and 75 and 100 had a bronze tank with gilt wreath.

The 1939 Wound Badge followed the qualifications for those issued in the Spanish Civil War; it was almost identical except that the helmet was modernized to resemble the 1935 pattern. It was worn on the lower left pocket below the Iron Cross First Class. Following the attempt on Hitler's life on July 20 1944, a special version of the wound badge was produced which bore the date and Hitler's signature below the helmet. Widows of those killed in the explosion received a badge in gold.

Just as armored troops received a combat badge, so too did the infantry. The *Infanterie-Sturmabzeichen*, introduced in January 1940, had a Kar98k rifle with fixed bayonet within an oak wreath and *Reichsadler*, and was awarded to soldiers who had taken part in three infantry assaults (including counter-attacks), armed reconnaissance, hand-to-hand combat or restoring a line on three different days. Initially, badges were silver plate over bronze but this was changed to zinc. A bronze version was produced for motorized infantry. The badge was worn on the lower breast.

A General Assault Badge was instituted in June 1940 for men who did not qualify for the Infantry or Armored Assault Badges. The *Allgemeines Sturmabzeichen* was in silver-colored metal and had a *Reichsadler* above a crossed stick grenade and bayonet, surrounded by an

FAR LEFT: A bronze *Panzerkampfabzeichen* which was introduced in June 1940 for members of Panzer-Grenadier regiments and medical personnel.

LEFT: The *Heeres-Flakabzeichen* (Army Flak Badge) was instituted in July 1941. It was awarded either on a bravery or points basis – 16 points being sufficient. Any AA battery which downed an enemy aircraft without support from other batteries received four points. Though the Luftwaffe received credits for targets destroyed on the ground, the army insisted that the badge was for air targets.

ABOVE: Black, silver and gold wound badges. A cloth version was also produced, possibly for wear on sports clothing. A special Wound Badge was made for survivors of the Bomb Plot against Hitler on July 20 1944. Produced in black, silver and gold, it had as additional features the date and the signature 'Adolf Hitler'.

RIGHT: *Infanterie-Sturmabzeichen* (Infantry Assault Badge) in silver and bronze. The *Allgemeines Sturmabzeichen* (General Assault Badge) below, was awarded to artillery, engineers, anti-tank, medical and anti-aircraft units that had supported infantry or armor. It went through grades from I to IV, ranging from 25 actions to 100.

LEFT: Himmler, Heydrich and Hans Prutzmann in the prewar black SS uniform.

BELOW FAR LEFT: An M43 panzer tunic and cap for an SS Hauptsturmführer in Leibstandarte SS Adolf Hitler (LSSAH); the owner holds the Knight's Cross as well as EK1, wound and tank attack badges.

BELOW LEFT: Reconstruction of an SS Hauptsturmführer of the 7.SS-Freiwilligen-Gebirgs-Division 'Prinz Eugen'. The collar patch shows the unit's 'Odal' rune which replaced the SS runes because the unit was non-German.

RIGHT: M43 helmet with SS runes.

BELOW: Kurt 'Panzer' Meyer of LSSAH gives orders during the invasion of the Soviet Union in the summer of 1941.

oak wreath. The award had been intended for combat engineers, but was expanded to include artillery, engineers, anti-tank and anti-aircraft troops who supported the infantry and armor in the assault. Conditions for qualification were to have taken part in three assaults on three different days. By 1943 four grades were added: Grade II bore the number 25 at the base, III had 50 and like Grade II, was in black with a silver wreath; Grade IV, the badges with 75 or 100, were not only larger but had a gold-colored wreath.

The badges were awarded retrospectively for service in Russia, back dated to June 22 1941, the first day of the Russian campaign. Eight months service qualified for 10 actions, 12 months for 15, and 15 months for 25 actions. So as John Angolia points out in *Military Awards of the Third Reich*, 'any qualified person who entered the Russian campaign on the first day was already qualified for the Grade II badge from the very day of its authorization.'

The *Nähkampfspange* (Close Combat Clasp) was intended for officers and men who had been engaged in hand-to-hand combat unsupported by armor. It fitted in place just short of the Iron Cross Second Class (EKII) and was struck in bronze, silver and gold for 15, 30, and 50 days respectively of hand-to-hand or close combat. If the soldier had been wounded in combat the qualifying days were reduced to 10, 20 and 40. A service-to-combat ratio retroactive from June 1941 credited five combat days as equal to eight months service, ten combat days, 12 months, and 15 combat days, 15 months. Hitler asserted that the *Nähkampfspange* in gold was just short of the Knight's Cross to the Iron Cross and he reserved the right to award it personally. By the end of the war a total of 403 gold Combat Bars had been awarded to men of the army, Waffen-SS, and Luftwaffe ground forces. The bar had a crossed bayonet and stick grenade with the national symbol above, and either side were oak leaf fronds.

A rather sinister badge, which was instituted by

FAR LEFT: An SS Rottenführer's jacket from the 3.SS-Panzer-Division 'Totenkopf' (Death's Head). The horizontal death's head collar insignia was introduced in May 1940; prior to that it had been vertical. It was based on the collar patch formerly worn by the SS-Totenkopfverfbande.

LEFT: Men of the SS-Kavallerie-Division during the invasion of the Soviet Union. In 1944 the division received the honor title 'Florian Geyer', and with it, the cuff title. From 1942 to 1944 some men wore an unofficial 'Kavallerie Division' sleeveband in Gothic script.

BELOW LEFT: A Sicherheitdienst (SD) senior NCO's cap. The SD was the intelligence arm of the SS.

RIGHT: The tunic of an SS-Schütze in 1.SS-Panzer-Division Leibstandarte SS 'Adolf Hitler'.

BELOW: A Waffen-SS M43 officer's cap with silver piping and, interestingly, a single button rather than two.

BELOW RIGHT: An Allgemeine SS senior NCO's cap. The black uniform went out of regular use when the war began and was replaced by field gray.

LEFT: Gunners in 12.Waffen-Gebirgs-Division der SS 'Handschar' (kroat. Nr 1). This Croat Muslim SS unit wore a green fez in the field and a maroon one on parade or walking out.

BELOW LEFT: SS feldmütze side cap, which was similar in design to that worn by the Luftwaffe and rather more stylish than the army cap.

RIGHT: Massed ranks of the Allgemeine-SS in a prewar rally. The SS or 'Schutzstaffel' – Protective Detachment – grew from a select group of 280 men who guarded Hitler.

BELOW RIGHT: An SS-Sturman with two Schützen of the Gebirgs Division 'Handschar'. As non-Germans they are not entitled to wear SS runes on their M43 tunic collars, but have the division's insignia of a hand holding a scimitar with a swastika. The men, who are Croatian Moslems, are reading a German language anti-semitic pamphlet.

There was some discussion in Nazi circles about the idea of forming an SS division which had an ethnic and religious basis. However, Reichsführer-SS Himmler stated that Islam was a good religion for warriors. The plan was to use the ethnic antipathy in Yugoslavia to pit Moslems against Serbian Communists in anti-partisan operations. In reality the men of Handschar were not the best elite troops.

WAFFEN SS

Eintritt mit vollendetem 17. Lebensjahr

kürzere oder längere Dienstzeitverpflichtung

Auskunft erteilt: Ergänzungsamt der Waffen-SS, Ergänzungsstelle V
(Süd), München 27, Pienzenauer Str. 15

LEFT: A recruiting poster for the Waffen-SS. The organization grew during the war years and its aggressive tactics and heavy casualties meant that there was always a demand for new men. The Waffen-SS began by trying to attract ethnic Germans from allied or occupied countries in Europe but were eventually forced to recruit non-Germans.

TOP RIGHT: Three SS-Hautptsturmführer who are identified as officers in the 23rd Croat Division 'Kama'. The officer in the middle may, however, be from Handschar prior to the authorization of the Croat armshield and distinctive collar patches. The officer on the right has the SA Sports Badge in addition to the *Deutsches Reichabzeichen für Leibesübungen* – the Reich Physical Training Badge.

RIGHT: Marksmanship lanyards; from left to right – the basic lanyard early pattern pre-1939; the basic award new pattern plaque; and the addition of at least one acorn as the marksman moved up a grade.

Reichsführer-SS Himmler in the last months of the war was awarded to soldiers engaged in anti-partisan operations. The *Bandenkampfabzeichen* (Anti-Partisan War Badge) was oval, with the inevitable oak wreath, but had a sword with sun wheel swastika thrust downwards into a swirling nest of five cobras and at the base a death's head. It was awarded from February 1945 onwards and incredibly, after the war, the West German government allowed the badge – without its swastika – to be worn by veterans of operations which had involved great brutality by both sides.

The army, Waffen-SS and Luftwaffe ground forces also qualified for three badges which were awarded as recognition of an individual's skill and bravery. The US Army Handbook on German Military Forces published in March 1945 suggests that awards like the *Sonderabzeichen für das Niederkampfen von Panzerkampfwagen durch Einzelkampfer* (Special Badge for Single-Handed Destruction of a Tank and the Close Combat Bar) were instituted because German troops were reluctant to engage in close combat. Looking at some of the citations for gallantry awards, particularly on the Eastern

Front, the reader is faced by a mixture of resolute courage in grim conditions and occasional moments of great valor.

To qualify for the Tank Destruction Badge a soldier had to knock out a tank using a Panzerfaust rocket grenade, hand grenade, mine or satchel charge. It required the nerves of a big game hunter to close with a T34 tank and push a Teller mine under the turret bustle, or cram a satchel charge through a hatch. The badge was worn on the right sleeve and consisted of a metal silhouette of a PzKpfw III on a silver lace strip with black borders. For every fifth kill a soldier received a gold-backed badge. The badge was instituted in March 1942 retroactive to the beginning of the war in Russia. The record for this type of anti-tank action was Oberstleutnant Gunter Viezenz who had four gold and one silver – a total of 21 tanks.

A similar type of badge was introduced in January 1945 for shooting down an enemy aircraft using a weapon of a caliber smaller than 12mm – this, in effect, meant the standard rifle or machine gun firing 7.92mm ammunition. In place of the tank there was an aircraft silhouette.

Though marksmanship lanyards, consisting of an aluminum thread cord with a plaque, had been introduced to the army in 1936, a Sniper's Badge was instituted in August 1944. The badge was in three classes and would have been awarded to soldiers engaged in the tough fighting in Normandy following the Allied landings in June 1944. The badge showed an eagle's head above oak

LEFT: An M43 tunic belonging to an Oberfeldwebel of Pioneers. It has the early dark green shoulder boards and full NCO tresse. The collar *litzen* are the second 1940 type, field gray on dark green with gray centers. Above the left breast pocket is the 1935-pattern eagle. Over the left pocket is the EK1 with a silver Wound Badge and the medal bar shows the 1941/2 Eastern Front Winter medal and EK2. The cap is an M43 pattern with BeVo eagle and *Reichskokade* woven in a single patch from rayon.

ABOVE RIGHT: One of the most recognizable features of the Third Reich, *der Stahlhelm* – the steel helmet. The M35 helmet has the tricolor shield in German national colors and eagle and swastika transfers; by the end of 1940 both transfers were being phased out and the helmet color, both inside and out, was matt gray. Helmet colors varied, however, from light to dark gray. The inside suspension to the helmet was leather and helmets came in five basic sizes weighing from 29 oz (0.82 kg) to 42 oz (1.20 kg). As an economy, the M43 helmet did not have a crimped edge.

BELOW RIGHT: The M16 helmet was used by the Reichswehr and, with the addition of helmet transfers, by the Wehrmacht. It was to remain in service with second line, foreign and civilian units up to 1945.

leaves and an acorn; Third Class was for 20 kills, Second Class for 40 and First Class for 60. If the soldier had confirmed 50 kills, he received 20 days leave and the Iron Cross First Class

Though the cut and quality of infantry uniforms deteriorated through the war, in 1939-41 the basic kit consisted of a steel helmet, a four-pocket field gray serge tunic with dark green collar and trousers tucked into marching 'jack' boots. Equipment was slung around a solid black leather belt which carried six ten-round ammunition pouches, a tent quarter, water bottle, 'bread bag', entrenching tool and bayonet, and gas mask in a metal container. A gas cape was often wrapped around the gas mask container, in part to keep the two essential items together, and in part to pad out the metal. The Waffen-SS were pioneers in the use of camouflaged uniforms. Smocks, trousers, tank overalls and helmet covers were produced in spring and autumn colors which involved complex printing patterns of up to three shades of green, brown and beige. The army and Luftwaffe paratroops adopted their own camouflage patterns, smocks, and uniforms, and although

FAR LEFT: A German infantryman in assault order negotiates barbed wire entanglements.

LEFT: An Obergefreiter wearing the EK2 and Winter 1941/2 medals, carries two Teller anti-tank mines.

BELOW LEFT: Marksmanship plaques and lanyards for panzer troops, with a gilt infantry plaque for recipients of 9 to 12 awards.

RIGHT: A Leutnant supervises a 2-cm flak crew in France in 1940. An Oberschütz readies the ammunition.

BELOW: An Unterfeldwebel with the Knight's Cross. He is probably the number one on a machine gun crew since he is armed with a pistol as well as binoculars and has the carrying case for the optical sights for the machine gun.

these garments were all intelligently designed, their variety reflected the empire building within the forces and lack of rational overall direction.

Equipment varied according to the weapon carried by the soldier, so if he was armed with an MP38 or MP40 sub-machine gun he had two three-magazine pouches attached at an angle for ease of access, and a similar configuration was produced for the MP44 assault rifle.

Other equipment would be a map case and binoculars if he was an NCO or officer. Officers could wear riding boots, and gray breeches with their field gray jacket, as well as a brown leather Sam Browne belt, although this made them obvious targets for snipers, particularly on the Eastern Front. In fighting in cities and built-up areas infantry would carry stick or 'egg' grenades to clear buildings and might be draped with belts of machine gun ammunition for the voracious M34 or MG42 machine gun.

Gunners, signallers and other support arms looked very similar in field gray except that they would be less heavily armed and further from the front line – as long as there was not a major breakthrough, when they could be called upon to fight as infantry.

To control troops and direct traffic the *Feldgendarmerie* or Field Police would be in position. They were recognizable by an orange embroidered sleeve patch showing the police eagle and swastika, but most notably by the metal gorget worn around their necks. This had a scroll with the word FELDGENDARMERIE and a *Wehrmachtadler* – both were painted in luminous paint, which meant that the policeman could be seen if he was on traffic duty where convoy lights had been blacked out. The police were not popular and the chain that suspended their gorget earned them the nickname 'chained dogs.'

ABOVE: The armshield, cuff title and gorget for the military police. The insignia on the gorget was in luminous paint.

LEFT: Field Marshal Fedor von Bock, who commanded Army Group Center in the invasion of the USSR in 1941. He is listening to a report from a Feldgendarmerie Oberfeldwebel.

RIGHT: Feldgendarmerie Unteroffizier's M43 tunic in the thinner summer-weight wool-rayon mixture. The collar *litzens* are in field gray with the orange *Waffenfarbe* of the military police. The Feldgendarmerie gorget was only worn when the soldier was on duty, but it earned the wearers the nickname 'chained dogs' by soldiers who suffered from ID checks by the police.

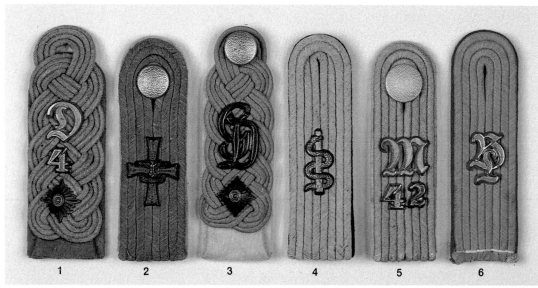

ABOVE: Epaulets and oak leaf collar patches of a Generalleutnant.

LEFT: Officers' epaulets. Staff (1); Grenadier (2); Infantry (3); Medical (4); Machine gunners (5), Artillery Observation (6).

BELOW LEFT: Army NCO and soldiers' epaulets. Ordnance (1); Afrika Korps (2); Infantry (3); Recruiting (4); Guard (5) and Veterinary (6).

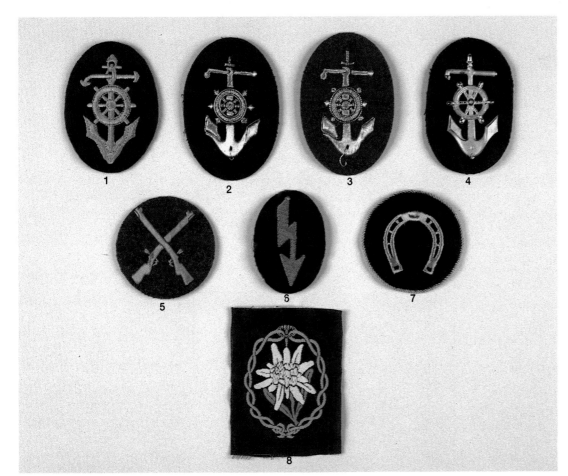

LEFT: Army Pioneer Assault Boat Helmsman (*Steuermann*) qualification badges (1-4). Ordnance NCO (*Waffenfeldwebel*) (5); Signals operators (*Nachrichtenpersonal*) (6); Qualified farrier (*Gepruftes-Hufbeschlagpersonal*) (7); Edelweiss sleeve badge for *Gebirgsjäger* (8).

BELOW LEFT: Army officers' collar patches (*litzen*). Chaplain (1); General Officer (2); Cavalry (3); Smoke Troops (4); Signals (5).

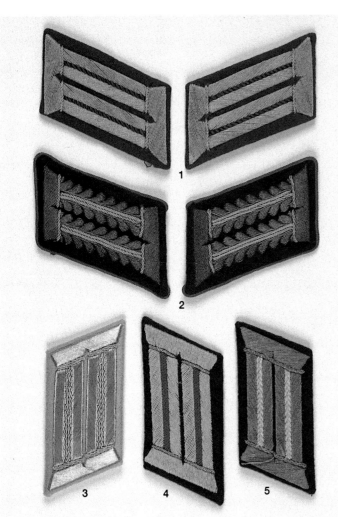

The army displayed rank on epaulets and collars with a system of colored piping and aluminum silver tape borders. Officers had 'pips' and sometimes metal numbers or insignia on their epaulets to show their regiment or arm. Infantry had white piping or *Waffenfarbe* (literally, arm color), cavalry and cyclist reconnaissance, gold-yellow; generals and artillery, crimson; mountain troops, green; panzergenadiers, grass green; medical, blue; engineers and construction troops, black; signals, lemon-yellow. When they were issued with camouflaged clothing, rank was displayed on the upper sleeve as a patch with green insignia against a black background. Trade and specialist skills badges were worn on the lower right cuff and were either letters or motifs: a horseshoe for farriers, or a lightning bolt for signals personnel for example.

In parade dress a colored troddel or sidearm tassel would be looped through the bayonet frog. Depending on the color, the soldier could be identified by rank, arm and even unit. Officers wearing the dress dagger or sword also had sword knots twisted through the guard. The officer's sword had the traditional lion's head on the pommel, and the *Wehrmachtadler* or *Reichsadler* across the guard. Other versions had etching on the blade showing, for example, horse-drawn artillery at the gallop or the *Wehrmachtadler* along the blade flanked by a Runic/Nordic design. Some sabres had motifs in base-relief on the langet, like cannon or crossed sabres. The Waffen-SS had similar swords, though in place of the traditional army motif they had the SS runes. The blade had the SS motto, MEIN EHRE HEISST TREUE – My Honour is Loyalty.

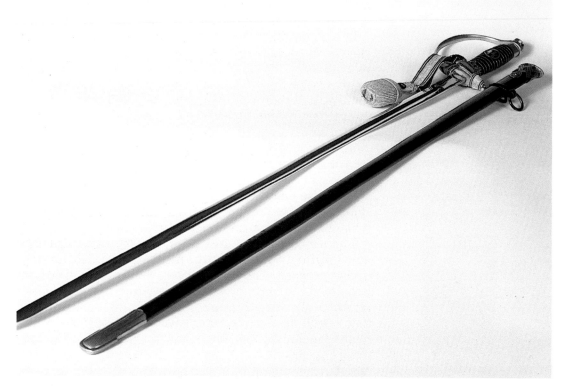

TOP LEFT: Dress tunic of an Oberleutenant in the Pioneers. The tunic is badged for an ADC at a headquarters and is a mix of parade and walking out dress. The aiguillette and medals are for parade wear only.

TOP: M43 tunic of an infantry Stabsgefreiter with Krim (Crimea) Shield, EK2 and Winter 1941-2 medals.

LEFT: SS Führerdegen graduation sword which was introduced in 1936. Given to company-grade officers, it has SS runes on the grip and silver aluminum sword knot.

ABOVE RIGHT: A medal ribbon bar with the Long Service Medal (blue ribbon) and Russian Front Medal beneath it. Reverse shows near right, obverse far right. The medal ribbon bar shows, from left Ek II; War Merit Medal, 2nd Class; Russian Front Medal; Army Long Service Medal; West Wall Medal.

RIGHT: Generalfeldmarschall's epaulet and collar patch.

The fighting in the extreme cold of Russia produced cold-weather clothing which was reversible white and camouflaged, as well as hats, mitts and boots. This was introduced only after men had suffered an appalling winter in 1941-42. Survivors of this grim phase of the war were awarded the *Medaille Winterschlacht im Osten 1941/2* – the 'Medal for the Winter campaign in Russia 1941/1942.' It was known ironically by the soldiers as the 'Frozen Meat Medal' and the criteria for award were: a minimum of two weeks of action (combat); 30 days over enemy territory for flying personnel; being wounded or getting a frozen limb, for which the Wound Badge was awarded; minimum of 60 days continuous service in the combat zone.

The service had to run between November 15 1941 and April 1942. Normally the medal was represented by a ribbon worn diagonally through the second button hole. The ribbon was red with a thin central white-edged black line. The medal was black with a silver border and topped by a helmet and stick grenade on the front was the national emblem; stamped on the reverse was WINTERSCHLACT IN OSTEN 1941/2 with a bayonet and a laurel frond.

Other campaign decorations issued to the German armed forces included the *Medaille für den Italienisch-Deutschen Feldzug in Afrika,* or Italo-German Africa Campaign Medal – either name sounds clumsy compared to the concise 'Africa Star' issued to British and Commonwealth forces. The Italo-German decoration had a ribbon in black, white, red and green combining the German and Italian colors. An Italian design, it showed the Axis allies as two gladiators holding closed the jaws of the British crocodile – this symbolized closing the Suez Canal. On the reverse was the Felini Arch flanked by a swastika and a fasces which was built by the Italians in Libya as a sort of triumphal victory arch. After Italy withdrew from the war and sided with the Allies, German veterans of the war in North Africa were prohibited from wearing the medal.

Campaign shields and cuff titles were a uniquely German decoration. The first shield to be produced was the *Narvikschild* for troops who fought at Narvik in 1940, followed by the *Cholmschild* for men who fought in the Cholm in 1942, and veterans of the tough battle for Crimea received the *Krimschild*. The Demyansk Shield, *Demjanskschild* was for survivors of the savage fighting in a 'pocket' near the small Russian town of Demyansk in 1942. The *Kubanschild,* or Kuban Shield was awarded to servicemen who had fought for 60 days on land, sea or in the air in the Kuban bridgehead on the Crimea in 1943. The *Lapplandschild* (Lapland Shield, 1945) was the last of the authorized shields to be manufactured and, interestingly, had a rather crude eagle

1

2

3

4

5

6

7

8

Osttürkischer Waffen-Verband der SS

9

ABOVE: An old-style army officer's cap with blue *Waffenfarbe* (Medical); the leather peak and softer crown as well as the embroidered insignia, allowed the cap to be tucked away when the wearer donned a helmet, and so it was popular as frontline wear with both the army and the Waffen-SS.

LEFT: Cuff title for army Propaganda personnel, which was instituted before 1939; army Field Post personnel received their title on September 29 1939; Unteroffiziervorschule titles were worn by staff and personnel at NCO training establishments and were instituted before 1939.

ABOVE: Infantry NCO's Schirmmütze (uniform cap) distinguishable from an officer's cap by its leather chin strap. In February 1936 certain senior specialist NCOs were permitted to wear caps with officers' silver cords.

LEFT: Crimean, Demyansk and Kuban armshields. The Crimea shield was instituted in July 1942 to commemorate the fighting in 1941-42, the Demyansk shield, instituted in April 1943, was for the defense of a pocket in Russia in 1941-42; Kuban, instituted in September 1943, was for the defensive battles fought on the Crimean peninsular after February 1943.

ABOVE: The dress cap for officers of SS-Brigadeführer and above.

LEFT: A M38 feldmütze with orange cavalry *Waffenfarbe* and the very distinctive Dragonadler badge traditionally worn by the regimental staff of 2 and 4 Squadrons of Reiter Regiment 6 and the 3rd Motorcycle Battalion.

TOP RIGHT: Army chaplain's cap with crucifix and purple *Waffenfarbe*.

RIGHT: Infantry officer's M38 feldmütze.

FAR RIGHT: The old and new caps worn by senior officers inspecting a foreign volunteer unit.

LEFT: A Luftwaffe NCO's tropical service cap, worn in North Africa by parachute air force units. It was a less common item than the Deutsches Afrikakorps (DAK) feldmütze.

BELOW LEFT: The DAK cap – shades varied from khaki brown to pale green. The *Waffenfarbe* indicates the wearer is in a transport or supply unit.

BELOW: On their BMW R4M motorcycle combination, DAK soldiers of a reconnaissance unit surge through the Libyan sand. In reality they would have covered their eyes and face against the dust – but this was probably a PK – propaganda company photograph.

RIGHT: Field Marshal Erwin Rommel visits a unit in North Africa. The field gray tropical service dress for many of these officers was probably privately made. Like their British adversaries, the Germans adopted a fairly relaxed attitude to dress in this field and even wore captured British and South African clothing and equipment.

without a swastika. The Warsaw Shield was to have been issued to troops who fought in Warsaw in the action against the Polish Home Army in 1944, but the manufacturer's dies were destroyed in an air raid and so it was never made. A Balkan Shield for troops who fought through Greece and Yugoslavia in 1944-45 was considered but not produced. The fortress ports of Lorient and Dunkirk, which held out until May 9 1945, had shields proposed but not manufactured.

Cuff titles showing regiments or battle honors had existed before the First World War. The Hannoverian 73rd Fusilier and 79th Infantry Regiments and 10th Jäger Battalion (who fought with British regiments in the 18th century) went into action against the British between 1914 and 1918 wearing the cuff title 'Gibraltar'. In the Second World War cuff titles were worn on the left sleeve, the first to be awarded being *Kreta*, for troops who had fought on the ground or in the air in Crete in 1941. An *Afrika* title flanked by palm trees was authorized in 1943 for surviving veterans of the Afrika Korps who had earlier worn a plain title with the word *Afrikakorps*. In 1944 after a long and heroic defense against the Americans, the German garrison of Metz were entitled to wear *Metz 1944*. The Courland pocket on the coast of Latvia held out against the Soviet 2nd Baltic Front from January 26 until May 9 1945 created its own cuff title which was made locally and had the shield of the Grand Master of the Teutonic Knight's Order and the coat of arms of Mitau flanking Kurland. The long defense of the pocket allowed the Kriegsmarine to evacuate casualties and civilians to Kiel and Denmark.

Kameraden auf See

A popular image for the film cameramen of the Propaganda Ministry in the early years of the war was the bearded and piratical-looking U-boat crews returning to bases in France after forays deep into the Atlantic. Laughing crew members were filmed receiving medals and war badges.

The *U-Boot-Kriegsabzeichen*, the Submarine War Badge, was issued from 1939 and was similar to the version produced in the First World War, except that the eagle and swastika replaced the Imperial Crown. The badge featured a U-boat surrounded by an oak wreath. It was awarded after two or three sorties. A combat clasp was issued from 1944 onwards which was similar to the army badge except that the center had a U-boat in place of the bayonet and grenade, and had slightly different oak leaves. U-boat crews received it on the basis of the number sorties or for personal bravery.

The *Marine-Frontspange*, the Naval Combat Clasp, was instituted in November 1944 and manufactured aboard the battle cruiser *Prinz Eugen*, so the quality of the workmanship is a little crude, It has an anchor flanked by oak leaves similar to other combat badges – there is no eagle and swastika. It was intended for crews who had displayed bravery beyond that which warranted the standard war badge.

ABOVE: A U-Boat commander and his first mate in the conning tower of their boat return from operations in the Atlantic. The officer wears the white cover on his service cap, which came to signify that he was the captain. The mate wears the naval version of the feldmütze.

LEFT: A U-Boat ace returns to a hero's welcome in Germany. He has removed the springing from his cap and wears the battle dress-style blouse top.

RIGHT: Naval officers flank a color party beneath a giant representation of the *U-Boot-Kriegsabzeichen* (Submarine War Badge) which was awarded to crews who had made two or more sorties or received wounds. The badge was produced in both gilt and cloth versions, the latter being more practical on board a ship.

A rather charming badge with the grim title of *Kampfabzeichen der Kleinkampfmittel*, or Combat Badge for Small Battle Units, had an almost cartoon-like swordfish with a reef-knot design. It was instituted in 1944 and awarded to divers, 'frogmen,' and one-man submarine operators. Both the Small Battle Unit Badge and the Submarine Badge were produced in cloth – far more practical if the wearer was on board ship.

The *Zerstörer-Kriegsabzeichen*, on issue from 1940, was for destroyer crews and was also issued to E-boat crews until they received their own badge, the *Schnellboot-Kriegsabzeichen*, from 1941. Mine-sweepers, Blockade Runners, Auxiliary Cruisers, High Seas Fleet, and Coastal Artillery received a badge based on an oval oak wreath topped by a *Reichsadler* and with a symbolic design in the center. The so-called Auxiliary Cruisers were better known as Commerce Raiders and were armed merchant ships, often banana boats, fitted out to attack Allied shipping. Appropriately the design showed a Viking ship.

Blockade Runners were merchant ships who undertook the very hazardous mission of breaking out of the Allied cordon around the continental European ports. Criteria for award included scuttling a ship to prevent its capture. The badge showed the prow of a liner with an eagle and swastika on the bows.

The High Seas Fleet War Badge, *Flotten-Kriegsab-zeichen*, was instituted in 1941 and showed the bows of a

ABOVE: The *Kriegsabzeichen für Minensuch-, U-Boots-Jagd-, und Sicherungsverbande* (Mine Sweepers, Submarine Hunters and Escort Vessels War badge).

LEFT: Navy sports vest emblem (1) and Marine Artillery breast eagle (2) with epaulets (3) and army-pattern collar patch(4) for general officers as worn by land-based senior naval officers. Naval units crewed coast artillery on the Atlantic Wall.

FAR RIGHT: A Kriegsmarine petty officer sounds the bosun's whistle.

ABOVE RIGHT: 'Sea Comrades', one of the many patriotic songs produced on postcards in Germany before and during the war.

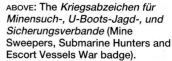

Kameraden auf See

Worte: Goet Otto Stoffregen. Musik: Robert Küssel.

Wir sind Kameraden auf See,
wir sind Kameraden auf See!
Drum, Mädel, nun gib mir den Abschiedskuß,
sei tapfer und treu, wenn ich scheiden muß.
Und fahren wir heute hinaus,
wir kommen ja wieder nach Haus.
Wir stehen wie Felsen in Luv und Lee,
wir sind Kameraden auf See!

Wir sind Kameraden auf See,
wir sind Kameraden auf See!
Der Flagge, die stolz uns zu Häupten weht,
ihr gilt unser Gruß, wenn's zum Sterben geht.
Sie ist unser heiligstes Gut,
wir schützen sie mit unserm Blut.
Wir stehen wie Felsen in Luv und Lee,
wir sind Kameraden auf See!

capital ship underway. Among the recipients were the crews of *Scharnhorst* and *Gneisenau* following the Channel Dash with the *Prinz Eugen* from Brest in France to Germany in 1942. The German capital ships posed a constant threat to Allied shipping and were the object of air and naval attacks.

Coastal Artillery were land-based naval personnel who manned anti-aircraft, search light and coastal defenses. They engaged incoming Allied aircraft as well as participating in the defense of ports that were raided by the British in Combined Operations Commando raids. On D-Day and in the months that followed June 6 1944, they fought duels with Allied warships conducting coastal bombardment missions. The badge showed an 8.8cm anti-aircraft gun.

The Minesweepers Badge showed the fountain of water from an exploding mine. It was awarded not only to minesweepers but also to submarine chasers and escorts; to qualify, crews had to have participated in at least three missions.

As the RAF Coastal Command and Royal Navy were joined by the US Navy, operations by the Kriegsmarine became increasingly hazardous and completing three missions a significant success. Recipients of the Navy War Badges also received a certificate. These varied from fairly muted documents to rather gaudy ones. The Germans were punctilious with these certificates or citations which accompanied all decorations issued to the three services and the Waffen-SS.

Naval uniforms varied from the conventional dark blue trousers, pullover top, and cap for ratings, and the double-breasted blazer and white-topped peaked cap for officers, through to field-gray army-style uniforms for

Coastal Artillery with rank displayed on epaulets. Naval shore personnel had a gold *Wehrmachtadler* on the right breast. White uniforms and khaki Afrika Korps-style uniforms were issued to ships crews or men in tropical shore establishments. U-boat crews had a range of clothes from ex-British battledress blouses, through to leather jackets and trousers – this latter kit was also acquired by Waffen-SS tank crews in 1944. In dress uniform the Navy had a dirk with a white or black grip; the pommel of the 1938 Regulation Model had a *Reichsadler*, while the cross guard carried an anchor design. This motif was also etched on the blade. A gold thread knot was looped through the guard.

Hitler had joked that he had a traditional army, a National Socialist air force and a Christian navy; in its insignia the Kriegsmarine managed to avoid the worse excesses of Nazi trappings. The naval command flags for General Admiral, Admiral, Vice-Admiral and Rear Admiral were all based on a Maltese cross design, with no eagles or swastikas present. The flag for the Commander in Chief of the Navy, *Admiralinspekteur*, introduced in 1943, retained the Maltese cross design, but with a gold *Reichsadler* at the center backed by crossed batons.

Land-based naval units had a dark blue flag with a white circle at the center and a gold oak leaf border; on one side was a swastika and on the reverse an iron cross. The swastika side had furled anchors and iron crosses in opposite corners, while on the iron cross side the two smaller iron crosses were replaced by the *Reichsadler*. A version of this flag was worn as a shield on the upper sleeves of naval flag bearers. On board ships the National War Flag was flown at the stern.

For every ship that took to sea or aircraft into the sky, there was always a vast staff of men and women who provided the administration and logistic support for fuel, ammunition and food, as well as pay, promotion and decorations. In addition, ships would require long-range communications which would also have to be encoded. Many women fulfilled their war work obligation in Germany doing this vital support work for men in the front line.

ABOVE LEFT: Kriegsmarine cap for flag officers; it has had the springing removed from the crown. Officers of the rank of Captain, Commander and Lieutenant-Commander had one row of oak leaves.

ABOVE: Junior naval officer's cap.

LEFT: Breast eagle from tropical uniform (1); a Torpedo Assistant Leader's arm badge (2); Combat Badge for Small Battle Units Grade 1, which went to men who crewed one man submarines or 'human torpedos' (3); Electrician 1st Class in tropical rig (4); embroidered High Seas Fleet War Badge which was instituted in April 1941 for crews who had served 12 weeks at sea (5); Chief Warrant Officer's epaulet for tropical uniform for shore based personnel (6); embroidered Destroyers' War Badge, awarded for a variety of criteria, including being wounded in action and even for 12 sorties without any enemy contact (7).

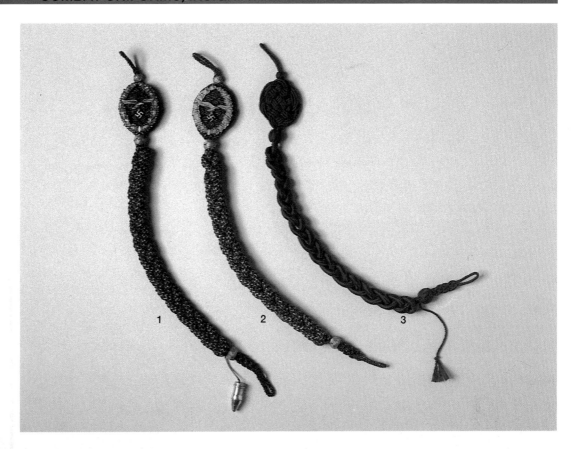

LEFT: Hitler visits the World War I battleship *Schleswig-Holstein* in Hamburg harbor.

BELOW LEFT: Rating's cap with the title 'Kriegsmarine' (War Navy) which, for security, replaced individual ship's names on caps in 1940.

RIGHT: (1-2) Luftwaffe AA crew marksmanship lanyards (a shell replaces the acorn which is on the army infantry lanyard) and (3) the Kriegsmarine lanyard.

BELOW: A Korvettenkapitan of the Line who holds the German Cross, inspects the crew of a small ship.

BELOW RIGHT: Grand Admiral Erich Raeder wearing the EK1 and medal bar from both World Wars, as well as the Nazi Party badge.

ABOVE LEFT: Naval anti-aircraft crew man a 2.0-cm flak gun on a warship. They wear helmets with the National Emblem, but no tricolor shield.

ABOVE: The practical side hat which replaced the older naval cap in 1940. The Edelweiss is an unofficial badge worn by some U-Boat crews.

LEFT: Grand Admiral Karl Doenitz with Korvette-Kapitan Schnee and Admiral Godt at the U-Boat operations section of the Kriegsmarine HQ in Berlin.

RIGHT: A wind-frayed Reichskriegflagge (National War Flag) streams from the mast on the conning tower of a U-Boat in the North Atlantic. U-Boats were able to surface run in the early years of the war when Allied air and surface patrols were not as effective.

Bomben auf Engeland

At the beginning of the war the Luftwaffe had enjoyed celebrity status in the armed forces. It had reduced casualty rates among the ground troops by assisting in the speed of their operations and, in Hermann Göring, had a charismatic and colorful leader. The Luftwaffe, unlike the army and the navy which survived the Armistice in 1918, was built from nothing in the 1930s by veterans of the First World War, some of whom were personal friends of Göring. He and they were keen to give it an identity and traditions, so new flags, uniforms and insignia were designed, many of which were seen for the first time in March 1935 when Germany acknowledged to the world that it had an air force.

Though the British like to assert that they won the Battle of Britain in 1940, for the Luftwaffe, the reduction in air attacks against the UK was not because they were 'defeated', but because the weight of their effort was redirected against the USSR in Operation Barbarossa. The Nazi propaganda experts produced a marching song for the air attacks on the UK – *Bomben auf Engeland* – Bombs on England.

The weight of the war swung against Germany and a bitter gibe from German soldiers in the field used to be 'Don't look at the sky, it belongs to the Allies'. Air raids on Germany put civilians in the front line and Luftwaffe day and night fighter aces became new heroes. The flak (anti-aircraft artillery) crews, radar, and search light operators included an increasing number of women as any available men were shipped out to the front lines.

ABOVE FAR LEFT: An Obergefreiter wearing the EK2 is helped into sheepskin flight overalls. The yellow backing to his collar patch shows that he is air crew or parachute troops.

LEFT: Hermann Göring heads a parade of senior Luftwaffe officers in 1940 in Berlin. In the front rank are Knight's Cross holders. In the background a tall RAD officer is visible.

ABOVE LEFT: A paratroop Gefreiter armed with a P.08 pistol and a MP.38 submachine gun during the tough fight for Crete in 1941.

ABOVE: Luftwaffe NCOs receive a briefing.

FAR LEFT: Luftwaffe NCO's cap with yellow air crew or paratroop *Waffenfarbe*.

LEFT: A fine quality officer's M43 cap with silver piping.

BELOW LEFT: Luftwaffe Signals NCO's tropical issue cap. Hot weather clothing was worn in Italy, Southern France and even parts of the USSR as well as North Africa.

TOP RIGHT: Luftwaffe tropical cap with embroidered insignia which made it more practical than the NCO's cap on the left.

MIDDLE: A fine example of a Luftwaffe staff officers' schirmmütze.

BELOW: The green piping on this Luftwaffe NCO's cap indicates that the wearer would be a member of an Air Security Field Unit or Civilian Air Traffic Control.

By the close of the war many Luftwaffe squadrons could no longer keep aircraft airborne and were pressed into service as infantry – which they regarded as practically a posting to a punishment unit. A civilian ATC or Field Security Unit NCO would be likely to find himself defending a grim river line facing the prospect of a Soviet assault.

ABOVE: Reichsminister Hermann Göring with his wife Emmy Sonnemann and Princess Olga of Yugoslavia at the opening of the Golden Gallery of the Charlottenburg Palace. Göring wears white dress uniform, as do Luftwaffe and SS officers in the background.

LEFT: Hitler and Göring with contrasting styles. Hitler modestly wears the EK1 and Wound Badge; Göring, his *Pour le Mérite*, EK1 and Pilot's Badge. However, Göring has not reached his full excess of decorations so this is probably about 1938.

RIGHT: A prewar photograph shows Hermann Göring, Benito Mussolini, Adolf Hitler and Count Galeazzo Ciano; behind is Minister Rudolf Hess, Reichsführer Heinrich Himmler and Field Marshal Wilhelm Keitel. The occasion is soon after the signing of the Rome-Berlin Axis (Axis Pact) in October 1936. Both Mussolini and Ciano wear uniforms with Fascist black shirts.

LEFT: Hans-Ulrich Rudel, the only holder of the Knight's Cross with Golden Oak Leaves, Swords and Diamonds, discusses tank-destroying tactics with Oberfeldwebel Herschel. The NCO wears the *Front-Spange für Kampflieger* (Medium and Heavy Bomber, including Dive Bomber, Clasp, with 400 sortie pendant) and EK1 on his jacket. He is holding a model of a Soviet T34 tank. Rudel was to amass 2000 sorties by the end of the war and received a special version of the clasp with the figure of 2000 in diamonds.

RIGHT: Luftwaffe Unterofficieren calculate a course during a navigation examination.

BELOW: A Ju88 Oberfeldwebel with the Knight's Cross poses in his bomber; he also has the EK1 and Bomber Clasp with 400 mission pendant.

The USSR, Italy and Germany had pioneered the use of glider-borne and parachute troops and in Germany these forces came under Luftwaffe command. It is hard to understand now how futuristic paratroops seemed in 1940 – their uniforms, let alone their mode of delivery to the battlefield seemed the stuff of science fiction. With dive bombers and massed armor they created the *Blitzkrieg* mystique. By the close of the war the paratroop arm was used exclusively for ground fighting which it conducted with distinction.

As can be imagined, the Luftwaffe had some ornate dress swords and daggers. Göring sported swords whose designs dated back to the Middle Ages, as well as more 'sporty' daggers. Officers and senior NCOs had a dagger with a white grip, silver thread knot and a Luftwaffe eagle as the cross guard. More interestingly aircrew and paratroops had a very practical gravity blade knife in which the blade was held within the handle. If a paratrooper or pilot was entangled in the shrouds of a parachute he could operate the knife single-handedly to cut himself free. The design reappeared after the war with a field-gray plastic grip in place of the wooden one for service with the West German Bundeswehr.

German air force uniforms were largely in a variant of the blue-gray color adopted by the British RAF at the close of the First World War. Like the Heer, the Luftwaffe adopted colored piping and backings to show to which arm of the air force the serviceman or woman belonged. Thus orange-yellow was the color of air crew and paratroops, red of anti-aircraft gunners, brown signals, blue medical and white the Hermann Göring Division, an infantry and armor force that received the patronage of its namesake. Air crew had a range of flight overalls and leather jackets and one Luftwaffe pilot shot down in France in 1944 fooled his French Re-

LEFT: Dress-quality Luftwaffe breast eagle (1); death's head collar patch from Panzer Division Hermann Göring (2); Hauptman's patch from the same division (3); artillery Obergefreiter in Hermann Göring Division (4). Though the division was well equipped and performed well, it was a luxury to set up and operate what was an army unit within the air force, and reflected Göring's desire to see the Luftwaffe attract some of the glory of the ground forces in the early years of the war. Also pictured are collar patches for Flakartillerie Leutnant (5); Hauptmann in Paratroops or Air Crew (6); Oberleutnant in Signals (7); Oberst in the Medical Services (8), and First Leutnant in the Luftwaffe Engineer Support Services (9).

sistance captors into believing that he was an Allied pilot because a leather jacket, silk scarf, gray trousers and boots – with no obvious German insignia – was the universal wardrobe of a fighter pilot.

Rank was on both the collar patches, where it was based on a symbolic eagle motif, and the epaulets, where it followed a more conventional style of pips and piping. The Luftwaffe also adopted sleeve rank for camouflaged or cold-weather clothing.

German ground and air crew had qualification badges which followed the basic oval oak and laurel leaf wreath design, though they had the distinctive 'flying' Luftwaffe eagle. Like army badges, they were worn on the left breast below the Iron Cross, and the time conditions for the award would be waived if the crew man had been wounded during operational sorties.

The silver-plated Pilot's Badge, *Flugzeugführerabzeichen*, had the eagle inside the wreath and was also produced in cloth and bullion thread for NCOs and officers respectively. A combined Pilot's and Observer's Badge was introduced in 1935. Senior Luftwaffe officers and foreign national leaders were presented with versions of the badge in gold and diamonds and the last recipient was Generalmajor Martin Harlinghausen in April 1945. Flugkapitan Hanna Reitsch, a remarkable female test pilot, was awarded a brooch version of the badge in gold and diamonds by Göring in person. Another interesting recipient was SS-Sturmbannführer Otto Skorzeny, presumably after the airborne rescue of Benito Mussolini from Gran Sasso in 1943.

LEFT: Qualification badges, some of which represented a skill learned, and some a combination of skill and operational experience. They were coveted and respected insignia. From L to R they are vehicle equipment administrator (1); armorer (2); Flakartillerie NCO (3); woven Pilot's Badge (also available in metal) (4); Air Gunner and Radio Operator's Badge (also available in metal 5); Parachutist's Badge (6) and a Luftwaffe eagle for wear on dress cloaks (7).

LEFT: Luftwaffe epaulets-signaller (1), airman (2), Feldwebel (tropical uniform) (3), Flakartillerie Feldwebel from 34th Regiment (4) and a Major from a flying instruction (Lehr) establishment (5).

BELOW LEFT: An Oberfeldwebel from a fighter squadron with the EK2 and a flying clasp.

RIGHT: The Luftwaffe flight blouse, which was originally designed for wear under flying overalls. It was cut short with a fly front so that buttons would not snag. The hip pockets were added to the design late in 1940 and the popular garment was widely worn, even at some ceremonial functions.

The blouse is badged for an Oberfeldwebel in the parachute arm and has an embroidered version of the paratroop qualification badge as well as the EK2. Paratroops wore the blouse under their smock overalls.

The Observer's Badge, *Beobachterabzeichen*, instituted in 1936 was in silver-plate with the eagle offset to the left in a watching attitude. 'Old' silver plate gave the eagle a subtly different appearance to the wreath. Like the Pilot's Badge it was also produced on cloth in thread and aluminum wire.

The *Fliegerschutzenabzeichen für Bordfunker*, the Radio Operator/Air Gunner Badge instituted in 1936, had a diving eagle clutching four lightning bolts in its claws. The swastika was at the base of the wreath – cloth and bullion thread versions were also produced. It indicated that the crew member had completed his training and conducted a minimum of five operational sorties.

An Air Gunner and Flight Engineer's Badge, *Fliegerschutzenabzeichen für Bordshutzen u. Bordmechaniker*, instituted in 1942 was similar to the Radio Operator/ Air Gunner's Badge, but did not have the lightning bolts. As the availability of raw materials declined, the quality of the construction of these badges deteriorated with the course of the war.

Military glider pilots were awarded a badge with a soaring eagle within the wreath, with the swastika at its base. Introduced in December 1940, the *Segelflugzeugführerabzeichen* was produced in aluminum.

A Flyer's Commemorative Badge was produced in 1936 for former aircrew. Pilots from the First World War were entitled to wear it and appropriately it showed an eagle perched with folded wings in an oak leaf wreath with swastika at the base.

The most evocative of the Luftwaffe badges must be the Paratroopers Badge, *Fallschirmschutzenabzeichen*. It showed a diving eagle with a swastika in its claws in an oak and laurel wreath. To qualify, a man had to have attended the parachute school at Stendal and completed his training and six jumps; to retain the badge a man had to re-qualify each year. By 1944 the tough standards had slipped and medical, legal and admi-

ABOVE: The tunic of a soldat in the Hermann Göring Division. He has the fliegerbluse and an M43 cap, and wears the Ground Combat Badge and Wound Badge in black.

LEFT: General-Oberst Wolfram Freiherr von Richthofen, a close-support dive-bomber expert, in conference in Russia in 1942. With him are two Knight's Cross Holders; the Oberleutnant on the left also holds the German Cross, EK1 and 2, and flying clasp. The older officer has the Pilot's Badge and EK1 from both World Wars.

RIGHT: Ernst Udet, wearing an early version of the Luftwaffe uniform with no breast eagle and a small 'political' eagle on his cap. He has decorations from the First World War.

ABOVE LEFT: A Luftwaffe Unterofficier's service dress with the Paratrooper Badge and EK1.

ABOVE: The M1940 tunic and M43 cap of a Flieger (air man) in an anti-aircraft gun unit. The tunic has the Luftwaffe Flak Artillery Badge and NSFK Glider Badge 1st Class.

LEFT: Luftwaffe Squadron cuff titles, one fighter and two bomber, named after First World War aces. This tradition is similar in style to naming warships after great admirals.

LEFT: Cuff title of the Regiment 'General Göring' (1) which transferred into the Luftwaffe from the Landespolizeigruppe General Göring in September 1935. Officer's cuff title for the Division 'Hermann Göring' (2), which was introduced in May 1942 following the expansion of the regiment to a brigade. The Afrika theater of operations cuff title (3) introduced for the Luftwaffe in February 1942.

BELOW LEFT: A Luftwaffe pilot is measured for flight equipment. He is wearing the one-piece flying overall over which a parachute and life jacket would have to fit.

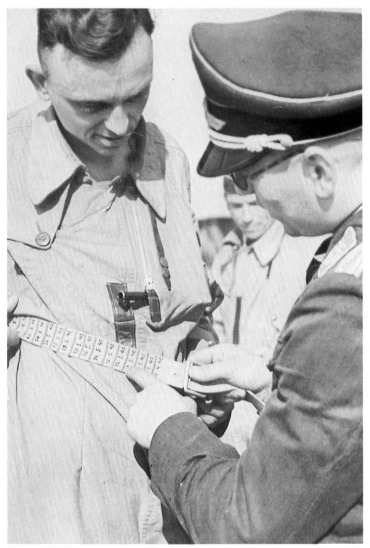

nistrative personnel who had made one jump were permitted to wear it. The original badges had the eagle in gold bronze and the wreath in silver. Materials changed with the war, but the colors were retained. A cloth version of the badge was produced in 1937 for wear on the jump smock.

The Luftwaffe had a range of operational flying clasps which gave an indication of the wearer's speciality – bomber pilot, day or night fighter, or reconnaissance pilot. They also showed how long he had been flying in skies which were becoming increasingly hostile.

In January 1941, after the Battle of Britain, Göring instituted operational flying clasps. Pilots, observers, bomb aimers, radio operators, flight mechanics, air gunners, war correspondents and engineers were eligible. The design was a laurel wreath flanked by oak leaves, with a motif within the wreath. From 1942 pendants showing the number of operational missions could be attached below the clasp. Originally three clasps were awarded, bronze for 20 operational flights, silver for 60 and gold for 110. The pendants were for 500 transport missions, 400 dive bomber or ground attack, 300 bomber, and 250 reconnaissance and night fighter sorties.

As the war progressed the clasps were further expanded and modified. The Day Fighter Clasp showed an arrow pointing downwards; heavy, medium and dive-bombers had a winged bomb pointing downwards; reconnaissance, air/sea rescue and met squadrons an eagle's head facing left; transport and glider squadrons the Luftwaffe eagle flying left; long-range day fighters and ground support squadrons a winged arrow, pointing downwards; long-range night fighter and night intruder squadrons a winged arrow pointing downwards

LEFT: An air crew or paratroop NCO's tropical dress cap.

BELOW LEFT: The *Erdkampfabzeichen der Luftwaffe*, (Luftwaffe Ground Combat Badge) which was awarded for close combat on the ground.

BELOW RIGHT: Paratroops at Narvik, where they landed above the Norwegian snow line and fought alongside the German mountain troops and sailors who had been pressed into service as ground troops.

RIGHT: The *Ehrenpokal für besondere Leistung im Luftkrieg*, (Goblet of Honour for Distinguished Achievements in the Air War). While not a decoration, this was an award for bravery and was for air crew members who have received the EK1 but whose actions did not merit the German Cross or Knight's Cross. This goblet was presented to Oberlt Horst Lohe in 1942 for reconnaissance flights.

within a black wreath; short range night fighters a winged arrow pointing upwards within a black wreath, and finally ground attack squadrons, which were initiated in 1944, had two crossed swords.

Like the army and the navy, the Luftwaffe had a range of war service badges. The *Flak-Kampfabzeichen der Luftwaffe*, or Air Force Anti-Aircraft Badge showed an 8.8cm flak gun at high elevation within an oak leaf wreath, with a Luftwaffe eagle at the top. Awarded to batteries who had downed sufficient enemy aircraft to have accumulated 16 points, it was instituted in 1941. The badge could also be earned by crews who had been involved in three successful ground actions, using the highly effective 8.8cm gun as an anti-tank weapon.

An Air Force Ground Combat Badge, *Erdkampfabzeichen der Luftwaffe*, was instituted by Göring in 1942. It had a matt-silver oak leaf wreath with a Luftwaffe eagle at the top, and below it a black cloud out of which a lightning bolt emerges. It was awarded to men of the Hermann Göring Division and to flak crews deployed in a ground role. To qualify, a man had to have taken part in three separate ground actions; as the war progressed, however, the numbers 25, 50, 75 and 100 were incorporated into subsequent designs.

As in the army, a Close Combat Clasp was instituted, which had a Luftwaffe eagle above crossed grenade and bayonet within an oak leaf wreath, flanked by oak fronds. It came in three classes – Class I for 15 days in close combat, Class II for 30 days and Class III (in gold) for 50 days. The first man to receive the award in gold was an NCO in January 1945.

In November 1944, at the same time that numbered Ground Combat Badges were instituted, an Air Force Tank Battle Badge, *Panzerkampfabzeichen der Luftwaffe*, was also introduced. It was available in two forms: either a silver or black oak leaf wreath surmounted by a matt-silver Luftwaffe eagle with a tank at the center. The former was for tank crew and attached medical personnel who had been in action for three separate days. The latter was for Panzergrenadier, armored reconnaissance, and medical units who had been in action on three separate days. The badges had the figures 25, 50, 75 or 100 in a box at the base.

An Air Force Sea Battle Badge, *Seekampfabzeichen der Luftwaffe* was instituted in November 1944 for air-sea rescue craft operated by the Luftwaffe . Within the oval oak leaf wreath was a symbolic ship with rigging and a smoking funnel. To qualify, crew had to have 60 days (10 hours at sea was a day) in the North Sea or the Mediterranean, Aegean or Black Sea.

Both the Luftwaffe and Hermann Göring had various types of flag or standard. As Reich Minister for Travel Göring had a Command Flag which had a red field with a silver laurel wreath within, flanked by stylised wings and containing on one side a black Imperial eagle and on the other a swastika. Beneath both wreaths was a *Pour le Mérite*. Black-edged bars radiated out to the corners and contained in each corner either an eagle or a swastika. When he became became Commander-in-Chief of the German Air Force in 1935, Göring adopted a standard with the Luftwaffe eagle in the center, but with the *Pour le Mérite* still displayed; on a later version he added crossed marshal's batons.

Ordinary Luftwaffe unit flags followed the army tradition of using the *Waffenfarbe* as the background color. On the front was a laurel wreath within which was the characteristic Luftwaffe flying eagle; radiating outwards to the corners were black-bordered white bars and within these, a black swastika. On the reverse was an Iron Cross within an oak wreath.

LEFT: A Luftwaffe feldmütze side hat with officers' piping but other ranks' badge.

BELOW LEFT: A Luftwaffe trumpet banner in paratroop or air force yellow. It is similar in design to the squadron or regimental colors. The reverse of the banner (top right) indicates that it is for the Schweinfurt Flight HQ.

RIGHT: A cap belonging to an employee of the Air Ministry in Berlin. The Bordeaux-red *Waffenfarbe* shows that he worked in an outlying building, rather than the ministry itself.

BELOW: M43 helmet with Luftwaffe decal. Helmets, like gas masks, were standard issue to all troops in the four arms of the Reich. The most common image of helmeted Luftwaffe personnel was the flak crews defending the Reich and occupied territories.

BELOW RIGHT: Car pennant possibly for the *Deutsche Luftsports Verein* (German Air Sports League).

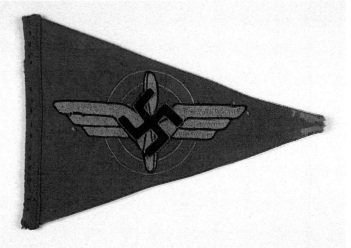

The Cross of War

A neck or chest order, a medal shaped like a Maltese cross and awarded for bravery in the field, dated back to the Prussian participation in the Napoleonic wars. In the Second World War the *Eisernen Kreuz*, the Iron Cross, became a yardstick decoration, and either side of it greater or lesser medals were instituted soaring to the heights of the *Ritterkreuz des Eisernes Kreuz mit Goldenem Eichenlaub, Schwerten und Brillianten* – the Knight's Cross to the Iron Cross with Golden Oak-leaves, Swords and Diamonds – only one of which was awarded by Hitler in person to Stuka pilot Oberst Hans-Ulrich Rudel in January 1945.

The *Kriegsverdienstkreuz*, the War Merit Cross, instituted in 1939, was for bravery and service not in direct combat and fell short of the Iron Cross. It was produced in two classes, with and without swords. The Second Class was in bronze and was worn from a ribbon. First Class was in silver and was worn as a pin-backed badge – the War Merit Cross with swords was for bravery and without, for service. One recipient was the Englisman William Joyce, better known as 'Lord Haw Haw', who was awarded the First Class Cross in September 1944 for his propaganda broadcasts to Britain. The first recipient of the First Class Cross was Dr Gustav Krupp von Bohlen und Halbach.

Almost in parallel with the development of the Iron

LEFT: The Grand Cross of the Iron Cross (1), Knight's Cross of the Iron Cross with Oak Leaves (2), Knight's Cross of the Iron Cross (3), bar to the EK2 (4), the World War 2 bar for the World War 1 Iron Cross (5), Iron Cross 1st Class (6) and Iron Cross 2nd Class (7).

ABOVE RIGHT: Iron Cross 1st Class with 1939 clasp to the 1914 Iron Cross 2nd Class.

ABOVE FAR RIGHT: War Merit Cross 1st Class in silver with swords for bravery – versions without swords were awarded to civilians.

RIGHT: Oberst Hans-Ulrich Rudel in the cockpit of an Me Bf 109, his Knight's Cross just visible at his throat.

FAR RIGHT: General Franz Xavier Ritter von Epp, interwar nationalist politician and founder of the Freikorps which did much to pave the way for the Nazis. He wears the 'Blue Max' as well as other decorations from the First World War. The imperial crown can just be seen on his EK1.

Cross, was the *Ritterkreuz des Kriegsverdienstkreuz,* the Knight's Cross of the War Merit Cross, instituted in 1940. Rendered in silver it was a neck order and was only awarded to personnel who had already received the War Merit Cross I and II. During the war only 118 with swords, and 137 without, were awarded.

The Honor Roll Clasp was a ribbon and clasp worn through the second button of the tunic. It was intended for men who, having won the Iron Cross First and Second Class, distinguished themselves further. Though the three services used the Iron Cross ribbon, the clasps were different: the army had a 'static' swastika within an oak wreath, the navy an anchor and swastika; and the Luftwaffe their characteristic flying eagle. Some 4,556 were awarded to the army and it is believed that 30,000 went to the Luftwaffe.

The War Order of the German Cross, *Kriegsorden des Deutschen Kreuzes,* instituted in 1941, was actually not a cross and neither was it in the line of succession of the Iron Cross series: it was the only medal to also be rendered in cloth. In metal it was a pin-backed star with a black enamel swastika as its central feature. Criteria for its award was bravery or service above the Iron Cross First Class, but not sufficient to merit the Knight's Cross to the Iron Cross. Interestingly it was

worn on the right breast, unlike the Iron Cross Second Class and other war merit badges. The German Cross in silver could be awarded for honorable military service for the war effort; in gold it was exclusively for combat. Both could be worn together, with the gold taking precedence. By the close of the war 30,000 German Crosses in gold had been rendered – 17,000 to the army and Waffen-SS – and curiously only 1200 in silver, 900 of which had gone to the army and Waffen-SS.

The Iron Cross Second Class, or EKII, *Eisernes Kreuz 2. Klasse,* was instituted on September 1 1939 for a single act of bravery. It was similar in appearance to the old Imperial decoration, but had a swastika in place of the oak leaves at the center and the date 1939 on the bottom arm of the cross. By the close of the war a total of 2,300,000 and Clasps to the 1914 EKII had been awarded. Some 39 women members of the armed forces received the medal. The 1939 Clasp to the 1914 Iron Cross was fixed to the ribbon when it was worn through the second button.

The Iron Cross First Class was identical in appearance to the EKII, but was pin-backed and worn centered on the left breast pocket. Awarded for three to five acts of bravery, the EKI and 1939 Clasp to the 1914 EKI were won by 300,000 servicemen.

FAR LEFT: Field Marshal Friedrich Erich von Lewinski von Manstein, wearing the Knight's Cross as well as the Imperial EK2 with bar, and the EK1 and bars for the Second World War. He appears to be wearing an additional Romanian decoration.

LEFT: Adolf Galland, the second pilot to receive the Knight's Cross with Oak Leaves and Crossed Swords; he also wears the Pilot's Badge, EK1 and Fighter Combat Clasp.

ABOVE: An embroidered version of the German Cross in Gold which was more practical on combat clothing.

TOP RIGHT: The pin-backed Iron Cross 1st Class (EK1).

RIGHT: Rudel, with the Knight's Cross and Oak Leaves, with his gunner who has the German Cross.

ABOVE: The award document for the Knight's Cross, which between 1939 and 1942 was hand lettered on white parchment. Hitler's signature was sometimes a reproduction, but where time allowed, it was original.

LEFT: The red leather folder for the Knight's Cross citation.

ABOVE RIGHT: The 1939 bar to the Imperial Iron Cross.

RIGHT: Possibly the last, and certainly the youngest recipients of the 20 million Iron Crosses awarded. These members of the Hitler Youth involved in fighting in Berlin, received the decoration in March 1945 at the Führerhauptquartier.

The Knight's Cross to the Iron Cross, or *Ritterkreuz des Eisernen Kreuzes*, better known simply as the *Ritterkreuz*, was instituted in September 1939. It was slightly larger than the EKI and EKII, and had a genuine silver frame. Criteria for the award varied – the Luftwaffe had a points system; the navy worked on a tonnage basis; for soldiers, continuous acts of bravery, or if a senior officer the successful conduct of a major operation. Like the EKI and II, the RK could be awarded to non-German pesonnel. The RK was a neck order and recipients often replaced it with an EKII when they were in the field. Recipients did not receive a full-length of black, white and red ribbon and so the RK was secured around the neck by a variety of means: Luftwaffe pilots favored attaching the ribbon ends to a girlfriend's garter.

Oak leaves, a device that had been adopted from the First World War *Pour le Mérite*, were added to the RK in June 1940, the first recipient being General Eduard Dietl after the fight for Narvik in 1940. In 1941 crossed swords were added to the oak leaves. Only 159 were awarded during the war. Finally, diamonds were added

in July 1941 to produce the definitive decoration – only 27 were ever awarded, the first recipient being the Luftwaffe ace Werner Molders. The single example of the Knight's Cross of the Iron Cross with Golden Oak Leaves, Swords and Diamonds was awarded to Oberst Rudel for his work against Russian armor.

Only one Grand Cross (1939) was produced and this was awarded to Göring for his leadership in the campaign in the West in 1940; it was, in effect, an oversized Knight's Cross.

When the war ended in 1945 with Hitler's suicide in Berlin, the whole Nazi structure began to collapse. The values, decorations and trappings suddenly became serious liabilities for their owners. The winter of 1945 saw trading for cigarettes in place of the now valueless Reichsmark and medals, too, became currency. Even courage had a price.

LEFT: On the terrace of the summer retreat at Adlers Horst (the Eagles Nest) at Ober Salzburg, Josef ('Sepp') Dietrich, transformed from a chauffer and bodyguard (see page 17) to a Waffen-SS Obergruppenführer with the Knight's Cross with Swords and Oak Leaves. Interestingly, among his other decorations is the Pilot's Badge. Dietrich, who served in the First World War, has a very impressive medal bar.

ABOVE: Following their successful operation against the Belgian fortress of Eben Emael, officers of the 1st Parachute Regiment receive the Knight's Cross from Hitler. In the center of the group is Oberst Witzig who commanded the group. They are dressed in parachute jump smocks.

RIGHT: Field Marshal Erwin Rommel in tropical uniform with the Knight's Cross with swords and oak leaves. His *Pour le Mérite* is not visible, but he has a full medal bar including decorations for service in both World Wars.

INDEX

Page numbers in italics refer to illustrations

Acknowledgments

Designer: David Eldred
Indexer: Ron Watson
Production: Nicki Giles

The author and publisher would like to thank a number of people for their invaluable help in the preparation of this book and for making their collections available for photography: Martin Windrow; Brian L. Davis; Militaria Consultants Ulrich of England/Andrew Steven/Peter Amodio; Malcolm Fisher of 'Regimentals', 70 Essex Road, London N1.

Photo Credits

BPL: 1, 2-3, 4-5, 6-7, 8 both, 9 both, 12 both, 13 top & right, 14 below, 16 both, 17 top, 18 below, 19, 21 both, 24 bottom, 25 both, 26 all 3, 27 top, 30, 31 top, 33 top right, 34 bottom

pair, 35 below left, 36 top left, 37 below, 38 below, 39 right, 40 all 3, 42, 45 bottom pair, 46 top, 48 left & below, 55 below, 58 top, 59, 62 top left, 65 below, 72 top, 74 left, 75, 76-7, 81 left, 82, 83 both, 88 top left, 89, 91 below right, 94 top, 95 below, 96 top right, 98 top, 99 both, 100, 104 top pair, 105 below, 117 below right, 118 below right, 119, 120 both, 123 top right, 126 top, 127 bottom pair, 128 top left & below, 129, 130 both, 131 both, 134 both, 135, 137 top, 143, 145 below, 146 below right, 150, 151 below right, 152 both, 156, 157 below.

Bundesarchiv: 6-7, 10, 11, 13 left, 14 top, 15, 17 below, 18 top, 20 both, 22-23, 24 top, 28 all 3, 29, 33 below, 43 top, 46 below, 47 below, 50 top, 51 below, 54 top right, 56 top and bottom, 64, 78 both, 80 top, 94 top, 121, 136, 151 below left, 155 below, 157 top.

Bildarchiv Preussicher Kulturbesitz: 34 middle pair, 35 top.

Brian L. Davis Collection: 27 below, 31 below, 32 below, 44 both, 45 top, 47 top, 48 middle, 51 top pair, 54 top left, 55 top, 56 middle, 58 below, 61 below, 62 top right, 63, 65 top, 67 below, 68 both, 69 both, 70 top, 71 top, 72 below, 73 both, 80 right, 91 top, 92 right pair, 93 both, 101 below, 104 below, 106 top, 108 all 3, 111 all 3, 112 both, 113, 114 both, 115 below, 122 both, 124 both, 125 below, 127 top, 138, 140 top, 144 below, 145 top, 146 bottom left, 151 top pair, 153 top pair, 155 top.

Henk van Capelle: 34 left pair.

E. W. W. Fowler: 32 top, 35 below right, 36 top right & below, 39 top left, 71 below, 80 left, 88 top right, 105 top, 106 below, 123 top left, 137 below, 140 below, 142 below,

153 both.

Regimentals (Floyd Humphrey Photography): 38, 54 below, 60 both, 61 top, 67 top, 70 below, 74 right, 95 top, 103 both, 110 top right, 117 top, 118 top, 125 top pair, 126 below, 141, 146 top, 147, 148 below, 149 all 4, 154 both.

Ulrich of England/Andrew Steven/Peter Amodio: 33 top left, 37 top, 41 all 3, 43 below, 49 both, 50 bottom pair, 52 all 4, 53 both, 57 both, 66 all 4, 79, 84, 85, 86, 87 all 3, 90, 91 below left, 94 bottom pair, 96 top left & below, 97 all 3, 98 below, 107, 110 below, 132 all 3, 133 all 3, 144 top pair.

Martin Windrow: 115 top, 116 both, 117 below left, 118 below left, 128 top right, 148 top.